Praise for
POSTCHRISTIAN

"Christian Piatt is one of the smartest and most provocative young voices we have."
—Jim Wallis, President and Founder, Sojourners

"POSTCHRISTIAN is written directly for the spiritual needs of the twenty-first century."
—Paul Brandeis Raushenbush, Executive Religion Editor, *The Huffington Post*

"I recommend this book to anyone of any religion who cares about a better, more compassionate world. Christian Piatt—one of the sharpest, most provocative thinkers in religion today—has written an important book full of righteous anger and profound mercy."
—A.J. Jacobs, *New York Times* bestselling author of *The Year of Living Biblically*

"For a profound book, it proved to be an easy read—but very disturbing."
—Tony Campolo, Professor of Sociology, Eastern University

"Touching, insightful, personal...Don't be deceived—the book is put in simple terms but it represents a powerful challenge."
—John D. Caputo, Watson Professor of Religion Emeritus, Syracuse University

"Piatt is no reactionary, wanting to save a dying institution, but neither does he take the popular route of simply walking away. Instead he believes that there is a subversive core in the tradition worth remembering and retaining."

—Pete Rollins

"Like the first rumble before a volcano explodes, POSTCHRISTIAN prefigures the revolution that will re-make Christianity in North America, and maybe the world."

—Frank Schaeffer, author, *And God Said, "Billy!"*

"Christian Piatt is right: behind the statistics of decline and the stories of dropouts is a platinum opportunity—one we Christians might never have seen or begun to seize if not for the wake-up call we've received."

—Brian D. McLaren, author,
We Make the Road by Walking (www.brianmclaren.net)

"Important, insightful, and timely...His words offer wisdom for a path forward and hope for the future of God."

—Matthew Paul Turner, author of
Our Great Big American God and *Churched*

"A powerful, reasonable book that takes an honest look at the Church's vices as well as its virtues in the hope that both the Church and its detractors can move beyond the zero sum game of 'us vs. them' and explore more constructive ways of living together."

—Kevin Miller, director of *Hellbound?*

"In POSTCHRISTIAN, Piatt gives us an operating manual for the faith of tomorrow."

—Jason Boyett, author of *O Me of Little Faith* and *Pocket Guide to the Afterlife*

"Don't read this book because you want to. Read it because you have to."

—Chris Yaw, founder, ChurchNext TV

"A new fresh take on the problems, possibilities, and potential of the original Christian message."

—David J. Lose, Marbury Anderson Professor of Biblical Preaching, Luther Seminary

"Not only does he connect dots like a pro theology nerd, but you can actually read the book without Advil and a dictionary."

—Tripp Fuller, founder, HomebrewedChristianity.com

"If you stick with [this book], really stick with it, hope, love, and imagination will blossom into a love-filled reality of what Christendom can evolve into: the Kingdom of God in the here and now."

—Rev. Phil Shepherd, aka The Whiskey Preacher

"Piatt peels back the dead wood of our faith and shows us the tender new life, reminding us of our core."

—Rev. Carol Howard Merritt, columnist for *The Christian Century*

Also by Christian Piatt

Blood Doctrine

Banned Questions About the Bible

Banned Questions About Jesus

Banned Questions About Christians

Split Ticket

PregMANcy

Lost

MySpace to Sacred Space

POST
CHRISTIAN

WHAT'S LEFT?
CAN WE FIX IT?
DO WE CARE?

CHRISTIAN PIATT

JERICHO
BOOKS ™

NEW YORK   BOSTON   NASHVILLE

Unless otherwise indicated, Scripture quotations are from the New Revised Standard Version Bible, copyright © 1989 National Council of the Churches of Christ in the United States of America. Used by permission. All rights reserved.

God and Anxiety bar graph courtesy of Tom Rees, Epiphenom blog: http://epiphenom.fieldofscience.com/2009/04/can-choosing-right-god-reduce-anxiety.html.

Missiongathering Christian Church's Apology Billboard created by and courtesy of Richard McCullen and Missiongathering Christian Church San Diego.

Jericho Books
Hachette Book Group
237 Park Avenue
New York, NY 10017
www.JerichoBooks.com

Printed in the United States of America

RRD-C

First edition: August 2014

10 9 8 7 6 5 4 3 2 1

Jericho Books is an imprint of Hachette Book Group, Inc.
The Jericho Books name and logo are trademarks of Hachette Book Group, Inc.

The Hachette Speakers Bureau provides a wide range of authors for speaking events. To find out more, go to www.HachetteSpeakersBureau.com or call (866) 376-6591.

The publisher is not responsible for websites (or their content) that are not owned by the publisher.

Piatt, Christian.
   PostChristian : what's left? can we fix it? do we care? / Christian Piatt.—First edition.
      pages cm
   Includes bibliographical references.
   ISBN 978-1-4555-7311-0 (hardcover)—ISBN 978-1-4789-5393-7 (audio download)—ISBN 978-1-4555-7312-7 (ebook) 1. Postmodernism--Religious aspects--Christianity. I. Title.
   BR115.P74P53 2014
   230--dc23
                                    2013050984

CONTENTS

INTRODUCTION

This book will piss you off, at least a little bit. It should, anyway. The Christian religion is not what it should be, what it claims to be. And whether you're a religious insider, a battered-and-bruised outcast, or a curious bystander, that should bother you. It bothers me.

But for every wound I expose, for every wrong I call out from the darkness into light, it's my hope that you'll find an equal measure of hope, love, and inspiration in the pages to come. There will be times when you want to set this book down for a while, or even toss it against the wall. That's fine; just don't walk away.

See, that's the problem. We find it all too easy to walk away when things get screwed up, when they let us down, when the divisions seem unbridgeable. But we owe it to one another to stick it out, to see more than one side to the story, to try, as hard as it may be, to see through someone else's eyes.

I'm not trying to get you to go back to church. If you're already in church, I'm not trying to get you to stay, any more than I'm trying to get you to leave. I don't care if you call yourself a Christian or not, if you've been baptized, offered the Sinner's Prayer, or proclaimed before a group of fellow believers that you've accepted Jesus into your heart.

I care more about the lives we're choosing to live, as individuals, as members of society, as churchgoers, skeptics, seekers, doubters, than I do about what you claim to believe or the institutions or groups with which you choose to identify. The labels just don't matter.

You matter.

For me, trying to model my life, my words, my ideas after a man I believe walked the earth about two thousand years ago is a personal choice. It's one of many, many choices. I don't need you to think like me, to believe the things I believe, for us to more closely resemble what I think we've been created to be. So call yourself a Christian or not, go to church or don't. But come to this book with open eyes, an open mind, and a willing heart.

I trust, as I hope you trust, that the rest will take care of itself.

CHAPTER ONE

LIONS AND LAMBS

SEEKING PEACE WITH THOSE WE HATE TO LOVE

Post-Christianity" is an often-misunderstood term. It means that today we live in a culture where Christianity is no longer the baseline for cultural identity and discourse.

We are witnessing the end of Christendom in the West as many have come to understand it: the dissolution of Christian hegemony. Some who value freedom of religion in a broader sense—or even freedom from it—view this favorably because it suggests that the stigmas and pressures against non-Christians are giving way to greater pluralism and tolerance, if not affirmation. Others who tend to view the United States as an essentially Christian nation point to a post-Christian society as the beginning of the end of Western civilization.

Secularists often cheer the decades of decline in mainline churches. Now, even evangelical Christian churches are experiencing similar declines; the retraction has reached all corners of Western Christianity.

On the other side, Christians are admonished to hold fast to their convictions, to defend God in our culture at all times and at all costs against the pervasive influence of mainstream media in our lives. The waning power of organized religion offers a clarion call to arms in the culture wars. Every slip in Christianity's status as cultural standard-bearer is viewed as dire news.

Frankly, both sides are out of line. Christianity can hardly be contained by religion, and in some cases, freeing it from the doctrinal limitations and economic encumbrances of the institution allows the faith to be more nimble, adaptable, and virally embedded in the culture in new ways. Yes, the Church has done damage, and yes, it is paying dearly for its own transgressions in the form of declining numbers and eroding credibility. But the heart and soul of Christ's message to the world was never bound to the institutional Church. Jesus spoke of liberation from bondage, justice for the oppressed, and sustenance for those in need. And yet too often, Christianity—and religion as a whole, really—falls well short of that ideal.

* * *

The onset of the post-Christian era might just be the timeliest opportunity for Christianity to be remade in the image of Jesus. For the last fifty-plus years, Christianity has occupied itself with justification and self-preservation, rather than humbling itself collectively before God and the world, welcoming accountability, and begging mercy for the countless historic and contemporary ways we have failed to faithfully serve the One we claim. Jesus would be calling us to account, instead of calling us back to the Church in its current state.

Jesus prophesied the destruction of the temple in Jerusalem, and maybe he'd join us in tearing down the walls of the contemporary Church until no stone was left, one on top of another. Or perhaps he might ride in on a cloud of glory, accompanied by bands of angels, to set Christianity right, placing himself at the helm of culture.

Or maybe he'd do something that no one would expect.

Maybe our idea of Church and Jesus' idea of Church are different, and we have gotten it wrong.

If, in the post-Christian era, we forsake the Church and all its flaws, we also risk losing much that it affords us. There are few, if any, other places in our world that place such emphasis and value on interdependence, story, unity, hope, justice, and radical, selfless love. We need these things, and Jesus knew that. We crave meaning, belonging, and community with others who bear witness to our lives. Rituals ground us. Symbols reach a deep part of us where language and reason often fall short. We need one another, even if we've forgotten how to be together in meaningful, vulnerable ways.

On the other hand, Christianity has been responsible for, or at least complicit in, some of the worst atrocities in history. The list is endless, and sadly, it continues to grow. Authority figures in churches prey on the vulnerable of their flock, we ignore the travesties of the world while planning another building extension, and politics are more important than people, just to name a few. The record seems to point to a toxicity in the Christian religion that humanity should endeavor to stamp out.

It's in basic human nature to choose sides in a conflict, to bifurcate the cultural landscape into "us" and "them." Jesus' followers believed him to be divinely empowered to conquer the emperor and fully expected him to lead a victorious revolution that would establish a new order. Instead, what they got was a suffering servant who died a criminal death. They didn't understand that Jesus came to serve as liberator rather than conqueror. Rather than wipe sin—or death, or corrupt systems of power—from the face of the earth, he pointed a way toward freedom from their power. But Jesus the Liberator and Jesus the Conqueror are very different in important ways.

A conqueror obliterates or oppresses the enemy. A liberator removes the enemy's power over its victim, with this result: both oppressor and oppressed must find a way to co-exist, living side by side in a world where they can no longer be content to label their enemy as "other."

This difference is crucial in our discussion of a post-Christian world because there is potential for greater division between those who seek to preserve the historical Church as it has been, and those who seek to remove religion from the cultural discussion altogether. The prophet Isaiah speaks of God's vision for humanity as one in which the lion lies down with the lamb. The lambs might feel it would be fair to turn the tables and have a go at the lions. That's not God's kind of justice. In contemporary culture, where secularists cheer the decline of the Church and Christians hold fast to their convictions in a perceived culture war, both see the "other" as lions, preying on their identity, seeking to destroy something they hold dear.

But if the lamb is liberated from the fear of being destroyed by the lion, the two must now engage in the hard work of learning how to live side by side. It no longer matters who is viewed as the predator and who as the prey.

But it's not fair, we say. We want justice, and all we're

given is peace! No wonder we killed Jesus. Would it really be any different today?

This book examines how and where Christianity, as an institution in human hands, has fallen short, and how its failings have contributed to the negative feelings so many have about the Church, both from within and beyond its walls. I want to see the Church reclaim its Christ-like vision, and become more closely modeled on the life and teaching of Jesus. I want to permit old things to die if necessary and, when possible, embrace the new visions to which God is calling Christians, non-Christians, and even those who do not claim a faith yet seek through their lives to heal some of the brokenness and inequity all around us.

Every other chapter is dedicated to what I've renamed the "seven scandals of Christianity": pride, certainty, lust, greed, judgment, fear, and envy. Each "vice" chapter is coupled with a corresponding chapter on a Christ-like virtue that serves as the vice's respective antidote: humility, faith, love, charity, mercy, courage, and justice. The vice chapters are roughly based on the seven deadly sins (pride, envy, lust, greed, gluttony, anger, and sloth) used by the early Church (and still referenced by the Roman Catholic Church today) to delineate the ways in which humanity consistently falls short of God's ideal for us. These have varied over time, but generally they offer an overview of the sinful nature of human beings. The seven heavenly virtues (chastity, temperance, charity, diligence, forgiveness, kindness, and humility) are those God-inspired and Christ-like ways in which we endeavor to overcome the brokenness of our humanity and close the gap between us and the Divine.

There are several reasons for the variance in my chosen

scandals and virtues from the original deadly sins and respective personal virtues. The Church tends to concern itself with naming, judging, and helping make right the sins of individuals, but here I want to apply a similar lens to the institutional Church itself. As such, some of the "sins" or scandals are not as pertinent as others without some adaptation.

In the final chapter, I evaluate what's left of the Christian faith and of institutional religion, whether we can fix it, and if so, clarify the "it" we're trying to fix. Unfortunately there are no "five easy steps to reinvigorating your church" at the end. But I attempt to answer the hard questions: Does fixing the Church matter? What is the endgame? Who are we doing this for and why do we care, when we consider that Christianity has, in a number of ways we will consider, brought us to this post-Christian age?

Like any good postmodernist, I answer questions like these reflexively, with "It depends..." followed by a handful of qualifiers to point out the cloud of confusion that stirs when we start having a conversation about "Christianity." Do we mean the Church as an institution? The faith itself? The spirit of Christ in our midst? For each person, the answer is a little bit different.

No matter how you define it, I think we can agree that Christianity is changing. We are in an in-between state. According to a recent Barna study, about 37 percent of the American adults surveyed, who identify themselves as Christian, actually qualify as "post-Christian" based on Barna's criteria.[1] Interestingly, the number increased to 48 percent for younger adults. Also included in the findings, posted on the Christian Century website,[2]

- 47 percent do not feel a responsibility to share their faith.
- 57 percent have not read the Bible in the last week.
- 33 percent have not attended a Christian church in the past year.

So a growing number of people who still personally identify as "Christian" do not ascribe to the traditional idea of what it means to be a Christian. Since we are no longer living beneath the shroud of Christian cultural dominance, it is still unclear where and how this faith that has endured through the centuries fits in a culture that resists stasis, labels, and many other values promoted by traditional Christianity. Where this shift will lead is unclear, but the destination is less important than the process of discernment itself.

CHAPTER TWO

THE GOSPEL ACCORDING TO KEROUAC

THE JOURNEY ITSELF IS THE POINT

*O*n the Road by Jack Kerouac is an epic tale of wanderlust set in the United States during the birth of jazz, one of North America's only original music forms. It was a defining book in my youth. I loved his pacing, the images he sketched with his words of bumping, smoky jazz clubs and Benzedrine-fueled treks across vast swaths of countryside. His style was hypnotic and vivid, and as a jazz fan myself, I could hear the songs he described being played by the jazz greats I idolized. But I hated the ending. More specifically, I hated that there was no ending. He and his entourage would blow through thousands of miles in a week, stretching from East Coast to West, only to turn around and do it all again in reverse.

What's the point? I thought. Nothing actually *happens* in the story.

It took more than a year for me to realize that the journey, and the adventures along the way, was the whole point. The novel captured the heated moments of ecstasy, the quiet hours of driving through the Nevada desert after a binge of alcohol and friendship. Kerouac, Ginsberg, and their entourage would be caught up in unexpected moments of indescribable beauty, the kind that transport us outside of ourselves, if just for a moment. The book was an impressionist snapshot of modern American experience, relationship, love, loss, tragedy, and adventure.

As a portrait of the human experience, *On the Road* is absent conventional frames of linear storytelling. I had unconsciously come to depend on those novelistic techniques, and when they weren't there, my first reaction was to try to articulate the plot, pin down the exposition, conflict, and resolution. But there were none. I felt rootless and unsteady reading Kerouac.

Once I surrendered to the idea that a story didn't have to have good guys and bad guys, didn't have to have a clear beginning, middle, and ending, didn't have to conform to a predictable formula, I enjoyed *On the Road*. My second time through it, I gave myself over to the momentum and rich imagery in the narrative. I was there, in the car with Kerouac, Ginsberg, and Burroughs. I sensed the music, felt the momentum, and experienced the volatility of his emotional reality. It was exhilarating.

Had I held the book to my standards for traditional story, I would have missed the point. I didn't realize that I was overlaying my expectations on Kerouac; only after his writing shattered those conventions did I realize they were constraining me to a set, fairly narrow way of experiencing the written word.

Kerouac's novels offer an opportunity to look at our lives and our stories differently. It can be frightening and infuriating, or it can be inspiring and liberating.

For centuries, we have looked at the Christian story in the

traditional, linear ways that I tried to apply to Kerouac. We want a *beginning*, a *middle*, and an *end*. The *end* for much of Christian theology has either to do with the status of your immortal soul after you die or, in a larger sense, the hastening of apocalyptic end-times, when God will rain judgment on humanity and will set everything right. Christians will be the good guys, the bad guys will be vanquished, and we will be rewarded for fighting on the side of the righteous.

It is part of our nature to organize and set guidelines. We all seek patterns in reality. We long to draw boundaries, categorize, label, and attach value to our encounters. In his book, *On Intelligence*, neuroscientist Jeff Hawkins says this about how the human brain works. It:

> ...receives patterns from the outside world, stores them as memories, and makes predictions by combining what it has seen before and what is happening now... Prediction is not just one of the things your brain does. It is the primary function of the neo-cortex, and the foundation of intelligence.[1]

Sometimes, however, how we use our brains to function in the world can also become a liability. A 2009 *Psychology Today* article called "A Hunger for Certainty" put it this way:

> Like an *addiction* to anything, when the craving for certainty is met, there is a sensation of reward. At low levels, for example predicting where your foot will land as you walk, the reward is often unnoticeable (except when your foot doesn't land the way you had predicted, which equates with uncertainty.) The pleasure of pre-

diction is more acute when you listen to music based on repeating patterns. The ability to predict, and then obtain data that meets those predictions, generates an overall reward response.[2]

This is, in part, why my wife sits up until 2 AM playing Candy Crush on her phone instead of sleeping, or why I nearly failed out of two classes in college because of Minesweeper. The predictability of such games is, quite literally, addictive. The certainty we experience from having a predictable reality yields a pleasurable effect, and it's that pleasure that we actually become addicted to. The pursuit of certainty is the way we get the pleasure we want.

The world we have to navigate is becoming increasingly less predictable. Many of the traditional categories within our culture don't seem to fit anymore, such as identifiers for race, political affiliation, and even the religious labels of the past. The more pluralistic and dynamic our culture becomes, the cloudier these previously distinguishable categories are. What if we find ourselves in a state of flux or transition—not yet here but no longer there—in which our dependable practices of making sense of things end up breaking down? How would we handle such chaos? Would it be chaos? What if we let go?

For decades, companies have depended on market research to figure out how best to promote, package, and craft their products. Billions of dollars are spent each year on far-reaching surveys, taste comparisons, and test audiences, all with the aim of creating a formula that we can use to reasonably predict the habits of a targeted consumer group.

Asking questions about people's likes and dislikes, or why

they prefer this brand of mouthwash, only reveals a fraction of a person's life. We tend to tell surveyors what we think they want to hear; sometimes we present what we want people to think about us, rather than what really motivates us. More often than we realize, we don't even know why we do what we do.

Many companies are now turning to disciplines like ethnography or cultural anthropology to try to understand our true motivations. Science indicates that observing people in their natural environment reveals much more about their preferences and habits than asking questions. In a March 2013 *Atlantic* article called "Anthropology, Inc.," a research company called ReD explains why they do market research in this seemingly unconventional way:

> ReD is gleefully defiant of those who want clear answers to simple questions, and prefers to inhabit a space where answers tend not to come in yes/no formats, or in pie charts and bar graphs. "We know numbers only get you so far," the company's website announces. "Standard techniques work for standard problems because there's a clear benefit from being measured and systematic. But when companies are on the verge of something new or uncertain...those existing formulas aren't easily applied."[3]

Something Is Emerging

It's helpful to first understand a little bit about the social and cultural dynamics that led to Christianity's place today. The post-Christian reality we live in is not simply the result of the failure of institutional religion to keep up with a rapidly changing culture around it. And though we find institutions to be a convenient—and often deserving—target, the reality of what has broken down is far more complex than the standard criticisms of Christianity.

The present approach of Emerging Christianity might well represent the salvation of the religion we rebuke and criticize. Emergents retool our approach, then create a more nimble network of communities that more accurately reflect the social dynamics of our fragmented, highly mobile, pluralistic culture.

The Emerging Church movement actively and sometimes deliberately steps away, in many cases, from the traditional hierarchic, institutional model of Church and instead builds intentional community with flattened models of self-organization. Technology is used not as another attraction tool gimmick, but rather as connective tissue to hold people together in new ways. The lines between where "Church" ends and "the world" begins blur in this movement, and the didactic, top-down impartation of faith-based lessons give way to conversations about how faith can be discovered, expressed, and lived out in daily life.

It is an overstatement to suggest that the shortcomings of our faith tradition are this simple, however. The problems go much deeper than failure of a religious system to maintain relevance in the world that surrounds it. Emergents may reorganize Church structures, present alternative models for worship, and even community, but this neglects some fundamental problems that must be considered in order to re-envision the faith.

MISREPRESENTING GOD

We Christians, we the Church, have misrepresented God and what Jesus calls us to be in the world. We have succumbed to the misapprehension that Christianity is primarily about what we believe. We have been experts in identifying people's longings, needs, brokenness, desires, and pain, but we have offered a false antidote. We have claimed that inviting Jesus as Lord and Savior into our hearts has an enduring, salvific effect that helps make the suffering and the longing go away. We have made the case that individual salvation is central to our faith, and that we can enjoy the fullness of God's presence by participating in life as prescribed by the Church.

The problem is that this is not what Jesus has asked us to do.

Our commoditization—and even monetization—of God as the solution to all of life's problems has caused us to be seen as peddlers of a snake oil cure whose lack of efficacy has been found out. The God we have sold from the pulpit, in the Sunday school classes, on television, radio, and now online is a false idol. And Christians purveying this blasphemously un-God-like God are among the last to realize that they are worshipping a golden calf.

I know this sounds heretical, and I will unpack this further soon. But suffice it to say for now that Jesus' ministry to the world was about so very much more than *feeling good*, whether in the context of worship, in daily life, or in contemplating the fate of our immortal souls.

Christianity has, for too long, promoted the false God of personal prosperity, while ignoring the reality that our lifestyles are built upon the backs and shoulders of those without power.

It's promoted the false gospel of the primacy of personal salvation, rather than focusing on making right the inequities and injustices, and emotional, psychic, and spiritual deficits from which so many suffer, keeping God's kingdom on earth from being realized.

It's made a false promise that a life lived in the spirit and path of Christ is one of comfort, perfection, and perennial happiness, when the very model for the Christian faith suffered greatly for the way he chose to live and even die.

We've suggested that acceptance of the Christian faith brings with it a sense of wholeness and peace, and yet we see brokenness and suffering all around us, and continue to experience it ourselves. We can't find and enjoy real peace when our neighbors are still suffering. Despite the prayers, worship services, Bible studies, and mission trips, we still must come to terms with our own incompleteness and longing, tugging at our hearts.

For some Christians, the answer is a matter of numbers. *We must expand our reach, broaden the Christian territory to bring the Good News as we understand it to those in need. Only then will God's love be complete and fully realized in this world.* This sort of "manifest destiny" approach to Christianity seeks validation in sheer numbers. If more people convert, we feel assured that we have, in fact, taken the righteous path.

Yet we all still feel inner deficiency. We still hurt. We still suffer. We, who are supposed to be the harbingers of the answer to all of life's woes, still fall victim to desire, pain, struggle, and a nagging emptiness that we were told would go away once we embraced the faith with our whole selves. But it hasn't gone away. Perhaps we simply don't believe enough. We haven't found the proper way to pray. We haven't submitted ourselves to the God offered to us on Sunday morning. Despite our best efforts, we must still be doing something wrong to feel this deficiency—and so our suffering grows.

Understandably, we're afraid to let go of our religion, even if it seems to be so terribly broken. We're afraid that, if we do, there will be nothing left. But the irony is that this release, this deep, complete, and humble submission, is the only way we can begin to truly understand how we've missed the mark for so long.

We've tried to fill a space within ourselves with God, but what if that space is, itself, God? We've confused comfort and ever-present fulfillment with our faith, but perhaps we, as people of faith, are not meant to feel whole, complete, content, and at peace. Maybe, in welcoming what we thought was God into our hearts, we actually have attempted to snuff out the very thing we sought. We are restless because our longing for God's kingdom to be realized is unfulfilled without our help. We are dissatisfied because we yearn for wholeness while still feeling unfulfilled. But the longing, the hunger, is the divine calling toward something more Christ-like, more like the world we pray for when we offer the Lord's Prayer: *Thy kingdom come, thy will be done, on earth as it is in heaven...*

Author, professor, and theologian Peter Rollins has written two books that are at the forefront of the postChristian conversation. In *Insurrection*, he reframes the crucifixion and resurrection of Jesus in a radical way. In *The Idolatry of God*, he continues this march, further making the case that we have misunderstood, at a fundamental level, God's place in our lives and what the life, ministry, death, and resurrection of Christ mean to our present existence.

At the heart of Rollins's argument is the idea that we all live with what he calls "the gap." No, this is not an innate attraction to affordable fashion; it is a deep sense of longing at the very core of our being. It is what drives us from the moment we are cut from our mother's cord. It manifests itself as a stark reality once we realize we are individuals in the world, separate from others. There is "I" and there is "other," and despite our efforts to overcome the space between, the distance persists.

We try food, alcohol, sex, material wealth, theological assurance, and anything else we can cling to that will rid us of this sense of deficiency or emptiness. And though each offers a temporary distraction from the persistent "gap," they do not solve the problem. The Church has become culpable when we claim to have the solution. We've presented our statements of faith, our doctrine, our rituals, our images of God as that key to release us from bondage. But still, we are enslaved by desire.

Whereas Rollins suggests this sense of absence is a gap, I would argue it is something less benign than what this term connotes. He contends that we have tried to fill this gap with false constructs of God, with ritual, prayer, and worship. But in doing so, we have created what he calls a "vending machine God." We sense our need, so we go up to the machine and make a personalized request. What comes out is a manufactured false god, one that is intent principally on making us comfortable, happy, and fulfilled, a god created in collusion between the Church and us. Much of the rest of the non-Christian world recognizes this to be a false idol, and millions within the Church have walked away in search of something more real, more authentic. It is one of the lynchpins at the heart of the shift toward a postChristian culture.

And so Christians have two choices: hold fast to these false gods we've come to worship and defend them against an increasingly—and rightfully so—skeptical world, or join in the process of tearing down the false idols, allowing the refining fires of God's inspiration to breathe something new into existence that may or may not resemble anything we've even imagined before.

For Rollins, it is only once we come to terms with the reality that the gap cannot be filled, that it is not our pre-ordained destiny as people of faith to be happy, comfortable and whole, that we can begin to find some peace with the less-than-perfect existence in which we find ourselves.

LISTENING TO THE HUNGER

Whereas Rollins's gap might simply be more of a vacancy, I understand it more as an idling engine. A hunger, if you will. We all live with this hunger, this sense that we can be more than we are, and the world can be better. We see injustices and suffering in the world, and we hear the call in our hearts to respond. We're restless, dissatisfied with "life as is." We need to *do something* about it. Hunger, after all, drives us to act. At its most basic level, it is self-serving. We hunger, so we seek out sustenance to satisfy the hunger. But this particular hunger is different. We have tried to feed it without success for a long, long time. It continues to gnaw at us until it quite literally consumes our waking hours, and even invades our dreams. Our hunger subsumes us and seems to threaten or destroy us. Understandably, we want to make the feeling stop. But in this case, the traditional stimulus-response transaction falls short.

If God is described as anything principally throughout Scripture, it is "Love." And I agree that God is love. But within love, there has to be a longing—a hunger—something that draws us out of ourselves and makes us willing to take the incredible risks that love requires. This impetus to love, despite the inevitable danger of it all, is the hunger I'm speaking of.

Psychologist Sherry Turkle recently published a book called *Alone Together*, about how the ubiquity of technology in our everyday lives is affecting how we relate to one another. While we are, in some ways, more connected to one another than ever before, we are also struggling with loneliness on what some might consider an epidemic level. Has technology made us lonelier? Not exactly, says Turkle. Nor has it become the panacea some might have hoped for in helping us to assuage our already-present loneliness. What the technology has done, she suggests, is keep us from coming to terms with the reality of what it means to be alone.

In an interview on National Public Radio's *Fresh Air*, Turkle stated that (and I'm paraphrasing here) if we can't come to terms with what it means and what it feels like to be alone, we will never experience anything other than loneliness. Unless we can begin to accept the fact that there will be times when we feel alone, disconnected from others, isolated, and find ways to be at peace with that sense of alone-ness, the resulting lonely feelings become a relative obsession, and seeking the antidote becomes an addiction.[4]

As such, the mobile phone in our pocket is the perfect false solution. We feel lonely, so we text a friend. We feel lonely, so we check Facebook. We feel lonely, so we send out a message on Twitter and wait for a wave of validation to come back our way in the form of a retweet, a "like" button, or a handful of words to assure us that someone out there still knows we exist.

But what this does in the long term is keep us from ever knowing how to be alone comfortably, to sit with absence and find ways to be at peace with it. So although the immediate connection that the phone and social media afford us may offer a stopgap quick fix, it actually ends up making the problem worse over time.

Comparing the need for finding peace with aloneness in order to liberate ourselves from loneliness resonates in large part with Rollins's call to embrace the "nothingness" of the gap. He urges us not to fill that space with falsely manufactured notions of God or anything else. Rather, we have to learn to exist with the emptiness in order for the nagging sense of loss that arises from it to lose its potency over our lives.

I believe this gap actually is more of a driving force in our lives than perhaps Rollins might contend. As with the idling engine mentioned earlier, without being engaged by the machinery around it, that engine has no real power. It simply consumes energy until the operator places the engine into gear and directs the potential energy into actual motion. I believe this hunger we recognize within ourselves is much like that engine. It has no particular will or agenda or sovereign power over our lives, although without it, we would be hard pressed to find any real meaning. It is the gap or the hunger that gives all of our actions purpose. Without it, we would remain in a state of perpetual inertia, content where we are without motivation to change anything.

We tend to see hunger in our culture of plenty as a bad thing, something to be eradicated, a problem that must be solved. But that is not the case with this particular hunger. As fewer and fewer people decline to recognize organized religion as critical to their lives, it's safe to say that our religion has failed to satisfy this hunger, though it has often claimed the power to do so. For decades, evangelists in our culture have sold Jesus as the solution to this hunger, and that by accepting him into our hearts, we will no longer experience such longing. But this is a false message. Truly, fully embracing the teaching and values of Jesus at the core of our lives causes us to be perpetually restless, discontent with things as they are. We see what could be: a world in which the hungry are fed, the powerless are raised up, and the oppressed are liberated. And until these things become reality, they haunt our dreams and they occupy our waking hours. We're compelled by a hunger to realize this kingdom vision in our everyday world.

We often choose to use that drive to help us seek a final solution, the panacea that will, once and for all, make the longing stop. But we need to accept that the hunger is an essential part of our nature and turn our attention outward to see where it might lead us. Where will we end up if we surrender? The hope is that it will lead us closer to God, closer to complete reconciliation with one another, toward a mending of all the brokenness and suffering in our midst. Will we ever actually get there? Theologian and philosopher John Caputo responds with a powerfully simple word to this question: perhaps.

HOW LONG? NOT LONG!

If we apply a similar dynamic to, say, the notion of "Thy kingdom come," in Jesus' "Lord's Prayer," we can begin to understand the purpose and place of this hunger in our lives. If we stand by and wait for God to come down from Heaven and make everything better, we are left with nothing but our present suffering to comfort us. We are weak, powerless, and worse, hopeless. But if we see the call of "Thy kingdom come" as a rallying cry for those discontent with the way things are, it is that dream upon which we rest and hang our hopes.

It is the *Way* toward which we orient ourselves, without the benefit of seeing the destination in the distance.

It is the *Truth* upon which the Commandment to love our neighbor with all that we have and all that we are is built.

It is the *Life* to which we are invited, one with real substance, real meaning, and yes, even real struggle, hardship, doubt, pain, and failure.

But in accepting the hunger as the still, small voice of God within us, in making peace with the restlessness, the sense of incompleteness, the "already–not yet" tension of living into a new thing still as yet not entirely imagined, we rob the hunger of its consuming power.

In accepting that God is the hunger, we avail ourselves to liberation from the power that hunger holds over us. We are freed from the confinement of our own selves and we begin, tentatively at first and with much trepidation, to learn what it means to live a life that is about so much more than being hungry.

Let's consider the possibility, at least for now, that as much as we've invested ourselves in the institution of religion, it never was the real point of Christ's Gospel message to begin with. Look at it fresh, with new eyes: apply new standards of measurement and bring new tools for observation and action along with us. If we focus principally on keeping our churches alive, we'll certainly be left behind.

When the rich man asked Jesus what he needed to do in order to inherit God's kingdom, Jesus told him to sell everything he owned. He didn't say this to everyone he met, but for this man, the trappings of his present life were shackles binding him, depriving him of the real life he claimed to want. Yet when presented with this stark truth, the rich man walked away, choosing to cling to his shackles, rather than take the key from Christ that would ultimately offer him his freedom.

We have to take a leap of faith into the unknown, trusting that, in doing so, we will find God in the process. We wait for God to reveal God's self in certain, satisfying terms that will settle and soothe our spirits. But as we can see in the story of Pentecost—the birth of the Christian Church—God's spirit is wild, chaotic, and even a little bit dangerous.[5]

In reflecting on ways to make this postChristian age one where we heed the call of Christ, I borrow a prayer from Kerouac himself, plucked from the words of *On the Road*: "Nothing behind me, everything ahead of me, as is ever so on the road."

CHAPTER THREE

THEN COMES THE FALL

THE CHRISTIAN SCANDAL OF PRIDE

Oftentimes, at the heart of pride in organized religion is a claim that we possess an absolute, immutable truth, and that we are charged with imparting this truth to the world. This is what some might call "propositional truth," which rests primarily on cognitive knowledge and the power of rhetoric. There is a right side and a wrong one: truth, and everything else. Differing sides engage in conflict to determine whose truth will prevail. And in most cases, it is the individual or group with the most power that overwhelms the other, claiming victory for those on the side of their version of what is right.

But in fact, they have simply been on the side of power.

There are several layers of pride involved in this kind of truth-claiming. First, there is the presumption that truth is "out there," somewhere, and that we have the capacity to capture it and claim it as ours. Christians sometimes do this with the Bible, poring over verses until every word is committed to memory. And though this is done as a spiritual discipline, and with the intent of better understanding and sharing the messages contained within the Bible, the sense of assuredness that the truth gleaned from the texts is the *only truth* can be used like a verbal salvo toward anyone who would claim something other than our understanding of what is right and good.

We tend to think of the Christian Church today as splintered, fractured along ideological, cultural, and doctrinal lines into thousands of pieces. But few people realize that early Christianity was actually broader in scope than the whole of Judeo-Christianity thought today.

In his book *Lost Christianities: The Battles for Scripture and the Faiths We Never Knew*, Bart Ehrman lays out just a handful of the many early Christian beliefs held by various factions in the second and third centuries A.D.:

> ...there were Christians who believed that God had created the world. But others believed that the world had been created by a subordinate, ignorant divinity. (Why *else* would the world be filled with such misery and hardship?) Yet other Christians thought...this world was a cosmic mistake created by a malevolent divinity as a place of imprisonment, to trap humans and subject them to pain and suffering.[1]

Some of these millennia-old debates still resonate within our faith conversations today. Some early Christians thought Jesus was both human and divine, while others thought he was entirely divine, and still more claimed he possessed no divinity at all. Some claimed Jesus' death was necessary for humanity's salvation, but there also were Christians who argued his crucifixion had nothing to do with forgiveness of sin. There were even those who said he never actually died at all:[2] sort of an ancient version of our Elvis sightings today.

The different schools of thought permeated the faith, dictating everything from which texts were sacred to how many gods there actually were. Many early believers were monotheistic, like most Christians today, but some claimed there were two, three, or even as many as 365 Christian gods.

The winner, so to speak, was a discipline of Christianity called proto-orthodoxy, which is sort of a great-granddad of modern Christendom. Those in power within the Christian faith deemed that their views were the one and only set of true Christian beliefs; all others who differed in any way were heretics, to be converted to the proper doctrines, or be extinguished. Out of this grew such modern tenets of the faith as baptism, the sacrament of communion, the concept of the Trinity, Jesus' joint humanity and divinity, and many other Christian identifiers still held as doctrinal truth today.[3] It was hardly an organic process in which some ideas gained traction while others faded into history. Instead, it was the adoption of this proto-orthodoxy by Constantine as the official state religion of the Roman Empire that led to its dominance over all others.

Those who differed in their views of the Christian faith were deemed to be heretics. Their leaders were exiled or executed, and all Christians were converted to the now-official state religion by force. As for Ehrman, he suggests that the importance of this proto-orthodox victory can't really be overstated. "A case can be made," he writes, "that this victory was one of the most significant events in the social and political history of Western civilization."[4] Aside from the new church-state alliance propelling the Roman Empire into greater global dominance at the time, the selected Christian views established during Constantinian rule have, arguably, affected more of our modern Western religious and cultural values than any other event in history.

And as victors tended to do throughout history, Constantine wrote himself into the Christian story. According to an April 6, 2012, *New York Times* article, Constantine saw himself as part of the fulfillment of apocalyptic Biblical Scripture:

> Once the empire had a Christian patron in Constantine, the meaning of Revelation changed again. For Constantine, after his own "vision," he himself was the conquering ruler for good, and the "dragon" of Revelation referred not only to Satan but also to Constantine's human rivals for the throne. Constantine later took heretics, schismatics within the church, and eventually even Jews to be the embodiment of the Evil One. Revelation had not lost its political power, but its political use had changed.[5]

In many ways, the establishment of proto-orthodox Christianity at the forefront of modern Western culture and religious belief is the ultimate illustration of "might makes right." Those who embraced this doctrine were promoted, favored, and empowered, while dissenters were labeled as apostates at best, and the embodiment of evil at worst. This was the birth of the faith that has dominated ever since, and it was this prideful, self-righteous ideology that fueled such unsavory distortions of the Gospel as the Crusades and the American concept of Manifest Destiny. From the venomous protests of Fred Phelps's Westboro Baptist Church to the "otherization" of those who stray from Church doctrine, similar hubris exists within the Christian faith today.

I Need No One

Pride is a curious thing. At its heart, it strives to present an image of strength, infallibility, and independence. Pride says, "I need no one," while the reality is quite the opposite. Lingering just beneath the façade of our pride is the smoldering sense that none of us is good enough. So we have a difficult choice to make—either we admit to the world that we are not the perfect spiritual figures we aspire to be, or we buy into our own deception, turning our backs on the hunger that nags at the core of who we are. We succumb to pride, the superficial sense of worth propped up only by a handful of external accomplishments, and a collusion of false perceptions.

A text from Proverbs comes to mind:

How much better to get wisdom than gold! To get understanding is to be chosen rather than silver. The highway of the upright avoids evil; those who guard their way preserve their lives. Pride goes before destruction, and a haughty spirit before a fall. It is better to be of a lowly spirit among the poor than to divide the spoil with the proud.[6]

Who wants to be lowly? Sounds miserable if you think about it. We'd much rather be admired, exalted, looked upon with awe and respect. But the call to lowliness is not a command to beat ourselves up, to tear ourselves down until our spirits are broken. It's actually a call to freedom—freedom from the endless cycle of trying to keep up the ruse, convincing the world we're something we're not. Freedom from being subject to the volatile, fickle opinions of others. Freedom from being valued simply for what we can do, rather than for who we are.

The author of Proverbs actually points to this in the first two verses of this excerpt, holding wisdom and understanding above the most precious trinkets the world deems important. Our value is no longer tied to the numbers in our checking account balance. It is bound to a deeper self-knowledge and self-acceptance. From this, the seeds of love for ourselves can germinate, cultivating an honest, unvarnished self-image that not only accepts the brokenness, the longing, the lack, and the hunger, but embraces it as a core part of who we are.

It may seem counterintuitive to consider that self-acceptance is first predicated on our ability to admit and accept our own lowliness. It's certainly countercultural. But the Gospel of Jesus is nothing if not countercultural.

THE CHRISTIAN PROBLEM OF PRIDE

Pride is ironic. Though my pride manifests itself by suggesting I am superior to others, it actually finds its roots in quite the opposite. Rather than being fed by a sense of legitimate righteousness, pride is rooted in a persistent sense of fear, doubt, and unworthiness.

Pride within the Church goes much deeper into the culture and history of our faith than any present headline-grabbing scandals might suggest. Early on in Biblical texts, we see humanity yearning to be singled out as God's elect; clamoring to be the favorite. From the early Israelites to current so-called "hyper-Calvinists," there are those who seek to set themselves apart from everyone else as particularly favored or beloved.

What begins, perhaps, as an effort to exalt the authority of God over the will of humanity can become a weapon of prideful judgment that we wield over others. We make plenary statements about the fallibility of our neighbors, while attempting to obfuscate attention from our own shortcomings.

Pride is not solely a Christian transgression, however. It is something we all possess to some degree and wield at our convenience when the need arises. For me, it was an effort to conceal the pain of my separation from my faith as a teenager that led me to prideful claims about the shortfalls of the Christian faith. And while some of those indictments ring true, the fundamental goal of my criticisms was to direct attention away from the fear that, ultimately, I might not be worthy of the Church or, perhaps, God's love.

However, the only way to live into the kind of love to which we are called is to lay ourselves bare. Rather than holding our faith out as the brass ring for which all should strive to feel whole and complete, we should make real our utter dependence on one another and on God. Instead of claiming to be God's favored or chosen people, we should look at the path of service, humility, and radical openness to which Jesus leads us. Rather than promoting the false notion that our faith satiates the hunger, we should confess our ever-present hunger, bearing up a portion of our burden for our neighbor to carry, while offering to do the same for them.

John Calvin, after whom the Calvinist religious movement was named, subscribed to the idea of "election." (It bears noting that the basis for the Church of England, the Presbyterian Church, and many others grew out of this movement.) Simply put, the idea originated with the claim that that there is nothing humanity can do to earn God's forgiveness. God and God alone deems whom to save and whom to condemn. Otherwise, human beings have agency in determining their own fate.

But for this to be the case, we have to introduce the theological idea of election, which says that God has preordained who will be saved and who will not before the dawn of history. It's written down in the Book of Life, so to speak, and it's done in permanent ink.

Returning to the idea of favoritism, the idea of God preferring some over others was hardly new with Calvin. The Israelites claimed to be God's chosen people, and in fact, many holy wars have been justified on this basis. Arguably much violence in today's world finds its roots—within a number of different religions—on claiming God's particular favor. In fact, many things can be justified when absolute sovereignty for God is claimed. Consider, for example, what Reformed preacher John Piper said in a video posted on his website, *Desiring God*, titled, "How Could God Kill Women and Children?"

It's right for God to slaughter women and children anytime he pleases. God gives life and he takes life. Everybody who dies, dies because God wills that they die.[7]

There is a curious but important shift that takes place when we claim that everything that has ever happened has been according to God's will. By claiming God as sovereign, we're actually putting ourselves in a place of humility, at the mercy of an all-powerful God. But the problem is that we ourselves are left to interpret what exactly God's sovereign will must be. This comes across as understandably prideful to those who don't hold such beliefs, particularly when we are boldly claiming God's judgment on others or showing preference for "our tribe" over the rest of the world. This kind of thinking also slips into the modernist trap of us-them, as if there were as clear a delineation in real life between "good" and "bad" people as God makes between the so-called sheep and goats in Scripture. Our pride becomes that much more glaring when we claim to know the mind and heart of God.

It's important here to clarify that not all who claim the teachings of John Calvin feel as Piper does, and that Calvinists certainly aren't the only ones within organized religion claiming to be God's favorite, chosen people. This is just one stark example of how Christianity comes across to the rest of the world when we make such bold claims about the sovereignty, favor, and will of God. Any number of natural disasters are attributed to the wrath of God, and in most cases, the ones suffering the brunt of that divine judgment happen to be the same ones particular Christians who maintain this image of God condemn as falling short of God's expectations. It's also worth noting that natural disasters disproportionately impact the poor, who are precisely those named in Jesus' beatitudes as having a special blessing in God's eyes.

I don't know about you, but if that's what it means to be blessed, I think I'll pass.

For example, after the massive destruction wrought by Hurricane Katrina, Pat Robertson of the Christian Coalition claimed that the deaths and loss of property were God's punishment for the sinful ways of the people of New Orleans. Liberty University's Jerry Falwell once said that "AIDS is not just God's punishment for homosexuals; it is God's punishment for the society that tolerates homosexuals."[8]

As author Anne Lamott famously said, "You can safely assume you've created God in your own image when it turns out that God hates all the same people you do."[9]

THE PRIDE DIVIDE

At its best, Christianity strives to help us become better people. At its worst, it diverges into pride, claiming its faithful are "better than." But claiming the message and following the call of Jesus is a humbling, vulnerable experience. We do not claim to have completed life's complex puzzle, but rather, we come to terms with the incompleteness of it all. We are lacking, we want, we yearn for more, to be more. We want to experience the fullness of love, but we're afraid that, if we truly lay ourselves bare, if we are vulnerable and transparent with our needs, the ugliness within us will crush our hopes for acceptance.

The world reinforces, on a daily basis, that to *need* is to be weak. People should not have to rely on anyone to make it through this life. We pull ourselves up by our bootstraps, lay claim to our own destiny, and live into that reality. Then, and only then, will we finally realize the peace and wholeness we really want, far beyond gold or silver, status or power, outside affirmation or superficial admiration.

This same expectation of self-reliance applies to the Church. As it turns out, Christians aren't any better than the rest of the world at admitting when we need someone beyond our typical, comfortable social circles. Instead we focus on buttressing our argument, affirming that we possess divine favor, and chasing after the feelings of validation that so much misleading theology continues to promise, hoping all the while that no one notices we're just as screwed up as everyone else. We, too, are frustrated with work, worried about our mortgages, feel guilty for not spending more time with our kids or more time trying to make the world a better place. The mandate of the Church is not to fix the lost and broken any more than it is a requirement of those seeking God to submit to the powers of the Church to impart such impossible solutions.

We will not find all the answers. We will not forever satisfy the hunger. But if we are to discover what life can be like without limping along with the crutches of pride to prop us up, we have to cast them off in faith, believing Jesus' claim which he made over and over, that it is faith—not perfection—that makes us well.

The world doesn't need another Christian in the sense that we've come to understand that word; it needs people who are seeking vehemently, individually and in relationship, what it means to be more Christ-like. Those of us within the Church don't know exactly what that means, but we've invested ourselves in covenant—a holy promise—to place this search above all others, including above the preservation of doctrine, the institutional Church, or our own sense of comfortable—but false—certainty.

Yes, the Church needs those who don't necessarily identify

as Christian, but not in the ways we tend to think. We don't necessarily need to transform them; we need to be transformed *by* them, by their stories, their questions, and their lives, as much as they need to be transformed by ours. But the opportunity of transformation is itself an act of faith, a gesture of trust that requires everyone, those within the Church and those outside of it, to be broken open and then "remembered" in a mosaic of body, story, heart, intellect, and spirit that hardly resembles the lives we cling to today.

But we can't begin to be broken open while also pretending to be capable of holding it all together on our own. We don't need to claim answers or confess truth to be faithful. In fact, such claims tend to have quite the opposite effect that faith has. We enter into the unknown spaces, exploring the mysteries together with all our reservations and doubts. But we do it together. This matters far more than whether the journey taken is on Sunday mornings or within the walls of a church altogether.

We won't be perfect at it, but the only ones expecting us to be so free of imperfection are ourselves.

CHAPTER FOUR

SPEAKING SILENTLY

THE CHRIST-LIKE VIRTUE OF HUMILITY

Every time I see a sign outside a church that says ALL ARE WELCOME, my guard goes up. Have the people inside really considered the full implications of what that means? Everyone in the world has an "other," some person or group of people we think less of than ourselves. We may parade around platitudes of inclusion and unconditional love, but there's someone out there we consider "less than."

For most evangelical churches, members of the LGBT (Lesbian, Gay, Bisexual, and Transgender) community are seen as the "other"; for liberal churches, it's usually the evangelicals. It brings to mind the scene in *Goldmember* when Austin Powers's dad says, "There's only two things I can't stand, and that's people who are intolerant of other cultures, and the Dutch!"

Though it may not be readily obvious to many Christians, much of the world considers followers of Christ to be, on the whole, fundamentally arrogant, intolerant, and judgmental. When my wife, Amy, and I wrote our coauthored book *MySpace to Sacred Space: God for a New Generation* (yes, now terribly dated by its title), we conducted a survey of more than 750 people who identified both as Christians and as non-Christians. In one section, we provided the prompt "Christians are..." and offered about two-dozen adjectives—an equal balance of positive and negative ones—then allowed people to select up to five that they identified with Christians on the whole. The number one answer, selected by Christians and non-Christians alike, was "judgmental" (78 percent chose this), followed by "hypocrites" (71 percent).

It's not so much that Christians who are perceived as arrogant need to make themselves feel better than others (though that's sometimes the case). Mostly it's about drawing some kind of boundary, defining one side as inside the line and the rest as outside. And, of course, those drawing the lines inevitably are on the inside. The Bible justifies these positions, and there is great comfort and affirmation in feeling included among the chosen few, rather than like the other poor, lost souls who must be made more like those on the inside. This is what most church members call the charge of the Gospel, but there is pride at the core of claiming propositional truth. We presume that we have something the rest of the world needs, never mind that they might have something to offer us, or that we might change in the process of engaging them in a meaningful relationship.

For many inside the Church, engaging in relationships with those perceived as different can feel threatening. It requires a vulnerability that we'd rather not risk. Instead, we find it more comfortable to cling to phrases like, "If you died today, where would you spend eternity?" or "Have you asked Jesus into your heart?" That way we have nothing to risk in the relationship. We maintain the power, the assuredness of salvation, and all of the vulnerability (and potential humiliation) rests on the other side of the table.

Meanwhile, the world has gradually turned its back on a faith that claims compassion without limit and love without exception, but that lives out those claims in ways that are anything but compassionate and loving. Why? First and foremost is fear. We fear change. Change requires us to release our grip on our propositional truth. It requires openness to the possibility that even our enemy might change us for the better. It's a humbling, disarming, vulnerable process, but if we're to model our lives on Jesus, it is the only way to come to know truth in any meaningful way.

Second, there is an ideological resistance among many Christians to entertain any perspectives deemed to be beyond the boundaries of proper Christian doctrine. This is because there is so much value placed in those delineations between us and them, or right and wrong, that any accession or even tolerance of outside "non-Christian" views is seen as a threat to the position being defended. A friend of mine, whose brother is a member of an evangelical Christian church, told me that he explained to her that he could not even sit down with someone who was gay and listen to their side of the story because in acknowledging their humanity by sitting down, face-to-face, they might misinterpret compassion for acceptance of their "lifestyle," which would compromise her brother's core Christian values.

Even Jesus experienced moments of humble transformation. Consider the story about the Canaanite woman who came to Jesus and asked for his blessing to help heal her afflicted daughter.[1] At first Jesus said no, and even referred to her as a dog. But as she persisted, Jesus was moved and compassion prevailed. He offered a blessing of healing and praised her persistent faithfulness.

Some who can't bear the idea that Jesus' heart was changed suggest he was actually testing the woman's faith. After all, if Jesus truly believed what he said to the woman at first, he was effectively admitting he was wrong by changing course. It also suggests that Jesus was, at least to some degree, a product of his culture. For some, this image of Jesus is far too fallible, far too human.

But if Jesus did know what he was doing, and if he was actually testing the Canaanite woman's faithfulness, then frankly, Jesus was being a jerk. Why test her and not all of the other people who asked for help? It makes more sense to me that Jesus' response mirrored what other people of his culture might have said to a Canaanite. His contemporaries saw Canaanites as less than human, and in as much as Jesus was a product of his culture, that was in him: good, bad, and ugly.

But what mattered most in the story was that his love for all of humanity superseded his prejudice and his cultural and intellectual understanding of what was right. His heart was turned in favor of love and compassion. But it was a choice. He had to decide to let love be greater than any of their differences.

That prospect scares the hell out of a lot of Christians.

It's easier to humiliate others than to be humbled. And Christianity, as many people understand it, can lend plenty of firepower if we are intent on humiliation. Break others down until they see the error of their ways. Reveal to them that they're sinners in the hands of an angry God so they come to God (through us) on bended knee, begging for the key to salvation. God has it, Christians offer it, and the rest of the world needs it. Most Christians who evangelize or otherwise share their faith don't set out to intentionally hurt, subjugate, or humiliate those they reach out to, even if the result is such. The problem lies in placing the ideology some Christians long so desperately to share with others over the humanity of that person that the potential for humiliation is born.

The essence of life is about allowing our biases and resentments to succumb to a radical love that tears down such boundaries. If we put this love first, even ahead of our own sense of righteousness, our personal well-being, and our own sense of what should happen, then we create the space necessary for the indwelling of God's spirit. We prepare a place for a love that knows no boundary and for a peace that passes all understanding.

We allow love to change us, whether it comes from Christians or not. If we truly believe that God is in all love, where we find it or from whom we receive it shouldn't particularly matter.

DOING THE TRUTH

When arguing propositional truth, there must be a winner and a loser. There is little or no room for compromise. After all, if we can be swayed to change our understanding of what is true even a little bit, then what we previously claimed as truth wasn't actually truth. So in staking out positions and waging ideological war with the other, we hold our truth as more important than the other with whom we are fighting. The loser of the argument, or the person in the *wrong* from the perspective of the person in the *right*, is dehumanized, and all manners of violence—emotional and physical—can be justified in the name of our truth.

It needs mentioning here that such claims of propositional truth are hardly the sole purview of the Christian right. Even within mainline Christianity, firmly held beliefs are deeply entrenched, cloaked in so-called truth which justifies the degradation of others, regardless of social, political, or theological leanings. It is a basic tenet in the nature of human beings. But so is sin. Just because something feels natural doesn't necessarily make it right. One of the biggest barriers to relevance in a world increasingly focused on plural coexistence is that we continue to fight so fiercely among ourselves about truth. Meanwhile others look on, wondering how in the world such a fractious lot is actually supposed to resemble the unified body of Christ.

Truth is not, in fact, propositional. It can't be encapsulated in an argument or justified with force. Saint Augustine of Hippo proposed the concept of what he called *facere veritatem*. This roughly translates as "doing the truth" or "making the truth happen."[2] For Augustine, truth is a phenomenon that is experienced at the deepest levels of human nature. It cannot simply be known on an intellectual level or preached from the pulpit on Sunday morning. It is experienced not so much within the pages of Scripture as within the bonds of human relationship. Yes, the Bible or a sermon may offer a spark, a glance through the veil as it were, at something that might be more deeply known as truth. But that experience, in itself, is not what Augustine is talking about.

It is only when humanity agrees to lower defenses, humbly laying down our swords and hammering them into plowshares, that real opportunity to experience such truth becomes possible. It is found in relationships, stories, family memories, and the very humanity of our neighbors. Truth is found when we reveal our own humanity to those we fear. In acknowledging the Divine in one another, brother and sister, we awaken to the realization that, in embracing our neighbor, we come that much closer to God.

That experience, in itself, is humbling.

HUMAN BILLBOARD

Two weeks after Amy and I arrived in Portland, we read that the annual Gay Pride Fest was taking place along the banks of the Willamette River. Within our new church community, we have ministry leaders, congregants, and supporters, some of whom are in various stages in their journey of discerning where they are with regard to sexual orientation. But Amy and I have seen, firsthand, much of the damage done by Christian judgment toward LGBT people. After working at Samaritan House, a transitional living facility for homeless people with HIV/AIDS, as well as at an open and affirming church (one that vocally affirms the inclusion of LGBT individuals, couples, and families within the Christian faith), it struck us that the majority of gay and lesbian people struggling with self-acceptance, or wrestling with suicidal thoughts, had some history of religious alienation or judgment at the heart of their story. As such, reaching out to help heal some of those wounds has become an active part of our ministry together. And sometimes it's as simple as assuring someone that they are loved.

It's one thing to tell people they are welcomed and loved,

or even to show them with action. But too often, even more open faith communities want only to look forward, without acknowledging the profound damage that has been done to so many in the name of God and their own faith.

As all of us learned back in kindergarten, saying you're sorry is a necessary step toward healing. It's not fun and can make us incredibly vulnerable, but it's that kind of vulnerable humility to which we are called both by the words and the deeds of Jesus. So why do Christians seem to have such a hard time actually doing it?

For some it's a matter of fear. They don't want to be judged, ridiculed, taunted, or singled out. Well, join the club, because plenty of folks have felt they were on the receiving end of such treatment by the Church for far too long. For others, it's a matter of accountability; they simply don't see why they should apologize for something they may not have done personally. But if we're truly all part of the same Body, if we're in covenant to hold ourselves mutually accountable, then when one transgresses, we all bear the burden of making it right.

That's why Amy had the sandwich boards made. They were based on a billboard a pastor friend of ours named Rich created and posted near his church in San Diego. I included the version of the image we used on the next page. We knew the second we saw it that the message was both brilliant and necessary. They nailed it. But we wanted to take it a step further. To physically wear such a sign around town, especially at a Gay Pride festival, is pretty disconcerting. People might laugh. They might spit at you or even assault you. Granted, we did have our kids with us, but if someone had particularly strong feelings about it, there's no telling what they might do.

AS A CHRISTIAN
I AM SORRY
FOR THE
NARROW-MINDED, JUDGEMENTAL, DECEPTIVE, MANIPULATIVE
ACTIONS OF THOSE WHO
DENIED RIGHTS & EQUALITY
TO SO MANY IN THE NAME OF GOD

After all, any true Christian knows that sticking with your convictions and carrying them with you, even when it's not convenient, can carry a very heavy price. But that's when it's most important.

It was a good thing that she had the sign placed both on the front and the back of her body, because some people didn't really want us to know they were reading it. They'd wait until we passed by, then do a 180 and gawk at the words in bright red letters.

We kept waiting for the first verbal salvo, but it never came. In fact, people started coming up and asking if they could take a picture. Some put their arms around her and had friends snap photos for their Facebook page like she was a celebrity. Others offered a quiet but heartfelt word of forgiveness. Some cried. Others gave her high fives. Some even stopped what they were doing to share stories about their own pain at the hands of Christians.

The whole experience was exhilarating, partly because it

started out being utterly terrifying. Too often we reach out, emboldened and armed with the truth, and with the full force and conviction of our church behind us. But that's not the kind of messiah we claim.

Yes, people called out to Jesus to save them, and he did indeed offer salvation. Just not in the way they had expected. They longed for a conqueror to ride in, kick ass, and take names, but instead he arrived as the Suffering Servant, vulnerable to the worst that humanity could bear to heap on him.

It was only in doing so that he could truly affirm his message that LOVE WINS. Other, more aggressive approaches might have had a greater short-term impact, but they would not have set the context for a faith founded upon the principles of peace, love, compassion, and reconciliation. I don't consider myself any kind of fundamentalist, but when it comes to the call of every Christian, it is the only way.

And at least on that one day on the riverbank in Portland, it worked. But it didn't work because Amy's gesture of humility and apology caused some kind of cognitive chain reaction throughout the crowd at the festival. It's not as if everyone's attitude about religion, Christianity, or even about her was changed forever in those moments. It was an experience of *facere veritatem*. Truth was experienced on a deep and personal level. It is a phenomenon we experience in our bones, one that resonates with our soul.

No one owned it. No one person held it over another. It wasn't even that the words on the sign Amy wore contained the basic truth that we experienced on that afternoon. But the words were symbolic of an act of submission, of humility, of a willingness to lay down swords, to erase lines of division and to step out into unfamiliar territory, despite the obvious risks. In experiencing this truth, this kind of deep knowing, this sense of peace beyond words, we experience what author John Caputo calls God.

For Caputo, God is not some abstract, propositional thing out there somewhere to be named, understood, claimed, and imparted to others. Rather, he makes the shocking claim that God, as we understand God, does not actually *exist*. Instead, God *insists*, so that all else might *exist*.[3] In this way, God is the impetus, the longing that draws us together. It is the desire for reconciliation. It is the mustard seed of hope that persists, despite our attempts to subjugate it with self-righteous claims of knowing the mind and nature of God.

God is the longing that is at the source of our strength needed for real, humble engagement of the other. It calls us out, just as it has called all we witness into existence. It is at the root of who we are, why we exist. It is a truth that can be experienced, and yet not entirely understood or even properly expressed.

In their book, *After the Death of God*, Gianni Vattimo, John Caputo, and Jeffrey Robbins put it this way:

> The name of a God is not the name of an abstract logical possibility but of a *dynamis* that pulses through things (*rei*), urging them, soliciting them, to be what they can be, and it is in that sense what is most real about them.[4]

We want to name God. We want to pin God down, to lay claim to God's essence and to possess it. But to do so is the very epitome of pride. For Vattimo, Caputo, and Robbins,

God is not a being to be named, but rather an "event" to be experienced, a process of becoming that for which we are perfectly made. It is experienced as part of an ongoing process, striving for justice, working for healing, and placing love for one another above all convictions of right or wrong that may be argued as the doctrinal foundation of our faith or even as the Biblical case for our beliefs.

We have to die to those old understandings of God and truth, or perhaps we must let those false truths, those false gods, die so that we might live more fully. God is in an apology, a gesture of humility, a healed relationship, and the gathering of a community. And this is something fundamental to who we all are, regardless of the faith we claim, the name or names we embrace for God, or our standing in our culture. It is a common, leveling, truly human experience to which we cannot lay claim, but in which we can all dwell.

It is the holy ground on which all of us can meet.

CHAPTER FIVE

HOUSE OF CARDS

THE CHRISTIAN SCANDAL OF CERTAINTY

Science and religion have a historically volatile relationship that far precedes the Scopes Monkey Trial. Some five hundred years ago, Nicolaus Copernicus stirred the pot with religious leaders by putting forth the radical notion that the earth revolved around the sun, rather than the other way around, in his book, *De revolutionibus orbium coelestium* (*On the Revolutions of the Heavenly Spheres*). In doing so, he raised the ire of Protestants and Catholics alike. John Calvin accused Copernican theory of attempting to supplant the Holy Spirit in people's minds and hearts. Martin Luther suggested publicly that Copernicus was a scientific rebel without a cause; some even reported that Luther called him a fool.

Some years after its publication, the Catholic Church suspended, and later edited, Copernicus's book, while astronomers and many others within the scientific discipline continued to embrace and incorporate Copernicus's findings into their ongoing work. In the early 1600s, Galileo was charged with heresy for advocating Copernican theory and was condemned to a life sentence under house arrest.

History is replete with these kinds of stories, wherein

someone puts forward a different way of thinking about God or the universe, and they are castigated or even punished for their heresy. Though we have all heard of the scandals surrounding Copernicus, Galileo, or even the Salem witch trials in early America, fewer know the story of Michael Servetus. Born in the sixteenth century, Servetus was the definition of a renaissance man. He was an accomplished scientist, mathematician, poet, and theologian and even dabbled in the field of medicine. His contributions across multiple disciplines were celebrated as genius, though at the time he was most known for describing, with remarkable accuracy, the inner workings of the human circulatory system.

Servetus's ideas were less welcome, however, within the discipline of religion. He created an uproar within the greater Church by presenting a non-Trinitarian understanding of Jesus, for which he was later charged with heresy and burned at the stake. Among his most vocal critics was John Calvin, who sought to "purge Christianity of such filth, such deadly pestilence."[1] When condemned to die, his sentencing statement accused that he had "obstinately tried to infect the world with your stinking heretical poison..." His executioners, then, were "desiring to purge the church of God of such infection and cut off the rotten member..."[2]

In his book *Hunted Heretic: The Life and Death of Michael Servetus (1511–1553)*, scholar Roland Bainton lays out why religious figures like Calvin felt justified in both judging and condemning the death of dissenters like Servetus in service of the Christian faith:

The severity of Calvin was born of zeal for truth and even concern for the victim. Death itself seemed to him not too harsh a penalty for perversion of the truth of God. Today any of us would be the first to cast a stone against Calvin's intolerance; and seldom do we reflect that we who are aghast at the burning of one man to ashes for religion do not hesitate for the preservation of our culture to reduce whole cities to cinders.[3]

It's easy to sit at arm's length and judge Calvin, Luther, and even Catholic leadership for such forceful condemnations of the different-minded thinkers of their time. And although we've generally moved past the public burning of heretics, we still have fierce lawsuits over conflicting ideologies such as creationism versus evolution. The battle for the welfare and minds of our children is at stake, as far as the litigants are concerned.

There's a single word in Bainton's quote above that warrants particular attention, especially for our purposes. At first, his use of the word "victim" is a little bit disorienting. For most of us, it would seem clear that Servetus is the obvious victim in this story, but for Calvin, at least according to Bainton, he was no more than necessary collateral damage in defense of a more vulnerable victim: Christianity as a whole.

Calvin's foremost concern was the preservation of a set of ideals that he felt were critical to the well-being and salvation of the Christian faithful. It was about much more for him and those like him than simply using force by any means to assert their righteousness; it was a war of ideas, a war for the hearts, minds, and souls of humanity. And in war, it is inevitable that there will be casualties.

GATEKEEPERS ON A FLAT PLANET

You're either a sheep or a goat; you're saved or you're not; you're headed for eternal salvation or an unending fate of suffering and regret. This extends to Scripture as well. Most of us will be fairly familiar with some variation on this time-tested religious platitude:

> *You either take everything the Bible says, word for word as literal truth, or the whole thing is worthless. You can't just pick and choose what you want to believe.*

There are plenty of exceptions within religion to this rule, but faith communities are nevertheless characterized by this idea, particularly to those on the outside. One of the primary jobs of religion, as seen by many people both within and beyond the Church, is to draw clear—and generally immovable—lines that distinguish acceptable behavior from behavior that contradicts God's rules for humanity. More than simply focusing on the behaviors themselves, though, many governing religious bodies go further, labeling people as "saved" or "condemned," pious or evil, largely dependent upon their interpretation of Biblical texts.

There's an upside for institutions that draw lines. For one, those on the inside of the lines rest on the assurance that they're living right, and that God's favor is sure to fall upon them. It also gives us a measuring stick which we can aspire to and hold ourselves against, noting the clear differences between us on the inside and those on the outside. Although the primary reason we do this is for a sense of personal reassurance, it inherently marginalizes those who don't measure up, so to speak. Our certainty, then, comes at a cost to others.

Our lines and boundaries also make the mission of the Church abundantly clear: we need to get all the goats lingering beyond the lines inside the circle, so that they, too, can enjoy the merits and privileges of sheep-hood. How does one get inside the circle? That depends on the rules established by the ones who drew the lines in the first place (hint: it wasn't God).

It's easy to see how much power this places in the hands of the Church, once its faithful agree that the institution has the authority to make such claims. This has gone on for centuries, particularly taking hold on a global scale during the Crusades, when representatives of European governments went to all corners of the world to conquer and subdue foreign territory. This was done with the blessing of the Church, and done in the name of Christ. The people living half a world away who did not subscribe to the rules of Church establishment therefore were savage heathens, and as such forfeited all rights as human beings.

It's not surprising that those with power usually end up making the rules by which society must behave, as well as the consequences for violating these rules. But when ideology is valued more than the rights of the individuals on whom the rules are enforced, the result is institutionalized violence.

Though it has waned in recent decades, religion maintains tremendous power within our culture, seen by many as the ultimate authority about faith and the Bible. For some, Church is the gateway to salvation itself. When an institution either takes, or is given, that much influence, there's a risk that individual rights will be abused.

The good news is that most systems that have any sense of their own demise begin to adapt before they become extinct. It seems that, although some churches react to the cultural shift by claiming they need to be more rigid in their doctrine, others understand that a new sort of conversation has to start taking place. Possibly the most important question for organized religion in the twenty-first century is whether it's more important to be "right," or to be Christ-like.

Instead of acting as servants, we've been acting as gatekeepers. Rather than stewards, we've become landlords. If the Church of tomorrow is to survive at all, it must loosen its grasp on the need to declare people as either right or unfit in the eyes of God. This new Church will come to accept that this is God's business and not ours. It will awaken to the reality that our place in the kingdom of God is one of humble service and compassion, seeking justice and empowering those without power, rather than interceding as judge and jury on behalf of God. We'll worry less about who people love than making sure they know they are loved. We'll spend less time tearing down and more time building up. We'll pay less attention to who is on the right path and focus more intently on walking the path ourselves, letting our actions and lives speak for themselves.

PRAY THE GAY AWAY

Eric James Borges was teased his entire life for being different. Though he didn't come out publicly until his sophomore year of college, he recalls emotional and physical abuse as far back as kindergarten for his differences. And though most children undergo some degree of hazing from time to time, the seeming indifference of the adults in his life made matters dramatically worse.

In a video recorded for the It Gets Better Project, an LGBT advocacy group focused on offering hope and community to LGBT people on the margins, Borges recalls being physically assaulted in a full high school classroom while his teacher stood by and watched.

The distressed teen had nowhere to turn at home either. He spoke of his Christian parents performing a ritual exorcism on him with the hope of "curing" him of his orientation. When that failed, they kicked him out of the house.

Though Borges went on to advocate for LGBT rights through the It Gets Better Project and through his work with The Trevor Project (a group committed to helping LGBT teens considering suicide), the demons of his past still lingered. Despite finding a community that affirmed and embraced who he was, the damage had already been done. He killed himself in early 2012.

Following is a quote from his suicide note:

My pain is not caused because I am gay. My pain was caused by how I was treated because I am gay.[4]

Is Christianity to blame? According to Eric, his parents loved him, and they thought they were doing the right thing. But like the case of Calvin and Servetus, there was a war for the future of Eric's soul underway, the cost of which was—at least as Eric perceived the actions of his church and family—his eternal salvation. Yes, the process of saving him from his otherwise indelible sins would be difficult, even dangerous, but his family believed his eternal soul hung in the balance.

The result was that a young man died because his life didn't live up to the expectations and mandates laid out by his faith. It's more than a little ironic that the same faith claimed by those calling for, or at least complicit in, the death of others is based on the life and teachings of another young man who was executed for his rejection of his culture's interpretation of the dominant faith tradition.

JESUS' RADICAL COMMANDMENT

Jesus came from the Jewish religious tradition, which was primarily governed by traditional laws, but Jesus was intent on placing a new law—that of the sovereignty of love—above all others. Most people have heard or read the so-called Greatest Commandment that Jesus imparted to those questioning him about Jewish law, but too often, the truly radical implications of his command are missed.

It was no small feat to be knowledgeable in these laws, which were central to the Jewish faith since the time of Moses, especially since there were 613 of them. Some are straightforward, such as keeping the Sabbath while others are more arcane, like not letting your cattle graze in the same field as other cattle.

Does God seriously care whether my cows meet other cows while having lunch in a field? And is it really an abomination to ignore this?

Though a lot of these laws may seem absurd to us now (like not wearing clothes made of blended fibers), collectively they were an essential part of the establishment of a social order among the Jewish people. Some were fairly straightforward moral laws; some were informed largely by their understanding of how the universe worked at the time; others were more like amendments to existing cultural norms; and others...well, suffice it to say I'm no expert on Mosaic law!

But as we humans are wont to do, some folks started assigning social standing based on people's understanding of, and adherence to, the law. People like the Pharisees and scribes, who knew the laws inside and out, sometimes held their piety over others, for which Jesus calls them to account:

> But when he saw many of the Pharisees and Sadducees coming to his baptism, he said to them, "Brood of vipers! Who warned you to flee from the wrath to come? Therefore bear fruits worthy of repentance, and do not say to yourselves, 'We have Abraham as our father.'"[5]

In other words, they were being self-righteous, simply because they were strict legal adherents and could claim Abraham as their forefather. So what! says Jesus. What mattered more to him was the intent and orientation of their heart. So if they were following the laws simply as a matter of tradition or personal pride, he had no use for them. And this wasn't the only time he leveled harsh words against the Pharisees and scribes:

> "For I say to you, that unless your righteousness exceeds the righteousness of the scribes and Pharisees, you will by no means enter the kingdom of heaven."[6]

So first he calls them a brood of vipers, and then two chapters later, he calls them faithless and suggests they may not inherit

God's kingdom. This was shocking stuff. It would be like someone today claiming that some of the holiest, most respected religious leaders of our day were the worst of the worst. Or perhaps saying the earth orbited around the sun. Or maybe even that they were gay.

In the Gospel of Mark, Jesus is speaking to a group of Sadducees, who were scholarly experts on the Jewish law. Interestingly, however, when a similar account appears in the Gospel of Matthew, he is speaking instead to a group of Pharisees, who were more like religious lawyers. It's not surprising, given the harsh statements made previously by Jesus about these men, combined with the growing adoration of the Jewish people for Jesus, that the Jewish religious leaders had a bitter taste in their mouths when it came to him.

In an account recorded in Matthew, the Sadducees see a chance to trip Jesus up. Their hope is to use the law to discredit him, to mock him before the people. As such, the Mosaic laws have become a bludgeon, and possibly even a justification for imprisonment and violence if he contradicts the law. But this gives the Pharisees and the Sadducees great power. They had the authority to condemn people for violation of sacred law. Although people sought wisdom and guidance from them, they were also men to be feared. In wielding the power of certainty with regard to interpretation of the law, they were the arbiters of who was faithful and who was unworthy. There was a clear line—defined by them—which none were permitted to cross.

Rather than taking their challenge on directly, however, Jesus confounds them the way he did, time and again. You'd think that, at some point, these guys would figure out they were outmatched! The Pharisees (as only lawyers can do) set a verbal trap for Jesus, hoping to make him look foolish in front of his new disciples:

> When the Pharisees heard that he had silenced the Sadducees, they gathered together, and one of them, a lawyer, asked him a question to test him. "Teacher, which commandment in the law is the greatest?" He said to him, "'You shall love the Lord your God with all your heart, and with all your soul, and with all your mind.' This is the greatest and first commandment. And a second is like it: 'You shall love your neighbor as yourself.' On these two commandments hang all the law and the prophets."[7]

Jesus looks beyond the specific details of the law, mining more deeply down to what is fundamentally at the heart of all the Mosaic laws: the law of love for God and one another. That was the point of the rules to begin with, although the Sadducees had turned them into something to glorify themselves and to control others whenever necessary.

Consider the text here from Mark 12:

> One of the scribes came near and heard them disputing with one another, and seeing that he answered them well, he asked him, "Which commandment is the first of all?" Jesus answered, "The first is, 'Hear, O Israel: the Lord our God, the Lord is one; you shall love the Lord your God with all your heart, and with all your soul, and with all your mind, and with all your strength.' The second is this, 'You shall love your neighbor as yourself.' There is no other commandment greater than these."

Then the scribe said to him, "You are right, Teacher;
you have truly said that 'he is one, and besides him there
is no other'; and 'to love him with all the heart, and with
all the understanding, and with all the strength,' and 'to
love one's neighbor as oneself,'—this is much more im-
portant than all whole burnt offerings and sacrifices."
When Jesus saw that he answered wisely, he said to him,
"You are not far from the kingdom of God." After that
no one dared to ask him any question.[8]

In this version, a scribe emerges from the crowd of flum-
moxed Sadducees to ask the same question posed by the
Pharisees in Mark. But in this case, he seems to be doing so
with a pure heart, truly seeking Jesus' wisdom and hoping
to learn from the law, rather than use it as a weapon. His
eyes are opened to the truth of Jesus' teaching. He under-
stands that there is nothing that can be placed before love. No
written law, however fiercely enforced, can affect a people so
powerfully as those whose sole focus is unconditional love.

Jesus sought to deconstruct this entire legalistic approach
to faith. He knew that if people truly put into practice the
command to love God and all others with all they had and
all they were, everything else would fall into its proper place.
Does that mean it would be neat, orderly, and easily governed by people in power? Hardly. In fact, at the heart of
radical love is a kind of anarchy, a leveling force that embold-
ens the meek and humbles the great. Rather than external
forces dictating the character of the people, the people themselves possessed all of the power they required to realize that
God's vision for "Thy kingdom come" was already in their
midst.

It's no surprise that his answers hardly satisfied those who really only sought to secure their positions as the elite and powerful among the Jews. And it wasn't even that Jesus sought to supplant them and put himself in their place, though many of his followers hoped he would. Instead, he turned the entire system on its head, stripping the law of its power to oppress, snatching authority from those with high social standing, superior education, or vestments of religious piety. He broke it apart, smashed the entire system into oblivion, and then handed out the pieces to everyone, so that, together, they might decide to re-create a social order governed by the love of which he spoke.

THE TRAUMA OF LIFE

There is one period in our lives when everything is more or less perfect. It lasts about nine months and it ends precisely at the moment that we draw our first independent breath, following our extraction from our mother's womb. During fetal development, we are held in perfect suspension. All of our needs are provided for; we are nourished, carried, incubated, and sustained in every way by our mothers. We want for nothing, and therefore, we do not have any responsibility except to grow. We don't even have to breathe or eat on our own. All is taken care of. It's kind of like Homer Simpson's Elysian Fields.

Then, in a flash of light and a shocking sting, our eyes open to a vast, disorienting new world. We take in air, gasp, and choke on the unfamiliar sensation. We are subject to variations in light and temperature, the effects of gravity, noise, and physical manipulation. Our food supply is cut off and suddenly we have to wait until someone chooses to feed us. We cry out wordlessly in need as the very first pangs of the hunger manifest themselves in us.

Religion throughout much of history has sought an antidote to this trauma that accompanies us since the day we are born. We long to return to that blessed assurance that all will be well, to re-create for ourselves a living womb in which we can enshrine ourselves, where all doubt, pain, want, and struggle will cease.

The orthodox Christian response to this hunger has been to offer certitude in the form of religious doctrine, proof-texted sermons, and other means of education. And although this was, and is, intended to embolden and empower, the result is that it inculcates its faithful with a false sense of peace. We establish a bubble around ourselves, holding at bay the vicissitudes and potential threats of the world. On the inside of the bubble, the religious womb, we are safe. We know all the answers. We know what is right and wrong, good and bad.

Unfortunately, this creates a binary relationship with the rest of the world. Everything either fits neatly within this religiously manufactured worldview, or is "other." And everything "other" is a threat. There are two options in dealing with this "other": convert it to our way of thinking or kill it.

This perspective gives rise to phrases like "spiritual warfare," as there is always a perceived threat "out there" to be fought against. Lines are clearly drawn and the winner takes everything. There is no compromise, no room for the possibility of change. There is only victory or defeat.

In my assessment, Eric's family was torn between a faith that placed their son outside the bubble and their love for him. Unfortunately as the story has played out in the public sphere, it appears that there was no leeway for him to be who he was and also be a part of the kingdom of God. The cost of that decision was the happiness, sanity, and ultimately, the life of a man who died still confident he was gay, but thoroughly unsure if he was loved. How, after all, can love be what it claims if first it requires you to fundamentally change who you are?

Is It Worth It?

Consider what the Church of today has become. We look to our religious leaders for the answers, divesting ourselves of our own divine birthright to seek out, wrestle with, doubt, and question the presence of God within the world and ourselves, in exchange for the illusion of certainty. We fear the unknown, find the wilderness of love without boundaries to be hard work, and sometimes even terrifying.

How will we know we're doing it right?

How can we ensure we will be loved back?

How much is enough?

What if I give all that I believe I have to give, and still there is unmet need in the world?

Such an act of incredible trust, to invest ourselves in the reckless, open-ended rule of love, would offer no certainty in return. Yet if we look into ourselves, if we look into the eyes of our brothers and sisters, if we seek to know the true meaning of it all, of why we are here, of what makes life worth living, we come back to the same answer, time and again: love.

Still we can't be sure. We shrink away from the faith required to love in the way Jesus displays, replacing it with doctrine, institutional authority, tradition, and intellectual firewalls that seek to confine life neatly within the pages of a book or within the safe, secure walls of the Church.

So we've done it once again. We have ceded control over our faith and our fates to those whom the Church endows to guide us. The problem is, not everyone is on board. Some see charlatans of religion, seeking only to amass power, for the hypocrites they really are. Some have invested their faith in these systems that have offered them supposed certitude, only to walk away with guilt, shame, and the same longing that sent them searching in the first place. Some simply never trusted the system. Whether out of shrewdness, laziness, fear, or an adventurous, independent spirit, they see no need for religion to intercede on their behalf in this search.

And yet, even for them, the hunger persists. We're inclined to seek the assurance elsewhere, forever grasping at that external solution to an unsolvable problem. But we are the ones who have made such vulnerability and longing into a problem. We don't want to appear weak. We might be taken advantage of, found out, cornered, and mocked, much like the Sadducees and Pharisees tried to do with Jesus.

This love Jesus offers can finally help loosen the grip on the desperate urge to return to the womb from which we were forced. But it requires an act of faith. We want to claim such faith while still clinging to certainty, but one can't co-exist with the other. We're uncertain of what that faith looks like.

In both Mark 10 and Luke 18, Jesus compares the kind of faith required to that of a child. The newborn, still growing accustomed to the utter shock of her new surroundings, clings to her mother's breast with a faith free of all pretense. A toddler takes its first unsteady steps toward his father, trusting only in the parent's love to overwhelm his fear. A daughter confides in her parents after having her heart broken, trusting not that they will fix everything, but that they will be there to listen, no matter what, and to love her in spite of the pain.

Is it worth it?

CHAPTER SIX

LIFE ON A FLAT PLANET

THE CHRIST-LIKE VIRTUE OF FAITH

There are many healing stories in the Gospels. Pastors talk about them in sermons, and teach them in Sunday school lessons. They are, for many people, the evidence they seek to prove Jesus' divinity. They believe that his power to heal is evidence that they must have faith in him as the Son of God.

But this isn't faith.

In many of these healing stories, Jesus says two things, over and over again:

And He said to her, "Daughter, your faith has made you well; go in peace and be healed of your affliction."[1]

And Jesus said to him, "Go; your faith has made you well." Immediately he regained his sight and {began} following Him on the road.[2]

And He said to the woman, "Your faith has saved you; go in peace."[3]

And He said to him, "Stand up and go; your faith has made you well."[4]

There are other examples, but the pattern remains. He tells the healed to *go* (i.e., do something with your new life), and he affirms that it is *their own faith* that has healed them. He also uses different words or phrases for this idea, as we previously saw, and there are many scholarly debates about the etymology of the specific words he is reported to have said. The point is that he turns the focus away from himself and back on them. It is their own faith that is the source of healing, wholeness, and salvation in their lives.

But faith in what?

It would have been so much easier if he had given them some sort of cut-and-dried "faith test" so they would know the things they must believe in so that they, too, could be made whole.

For Jesus, the people he ministered to had faith that was self-evident in their actions. The very fact that they took the risk to step out, reach out, and call out to him was the faith he was talking about. It could not be defined as a position on a certain set of beliefs. Rather, it was the act of trusting something greater than themselves that held any real healing power.

Such faith cannot be argued or defended; it can only be lived out. Today, many Christians have mistaken what it means to have faith, and have strayed far from Jesus' own example. All of us are encouraged by religious leaders to take a "leap of faith," as if we can make such a leap once we have mustered sufficient faith. Interestingly, the phrase "leap of faith" is often mistakenly attributed to Christian scholar and philosopher Søren Kierkegaard, whose original phrase was a call for people to take a "leap to faith." Oh, what a difference such a small word can make!

For Kierkegaard, the leap *to* faith is not something simply resolved internally. It is not about getting a certain set of theological ideas cognitively right or rhetorically taking a position before a congregation of peers. Rather, Kierkegaard's leap to faith is our response to a deeper call. In his book *Concluding Unscientific Postscript to Philosophical Fragments*, he explains this call-and-response relationship:

> The externality is the watchman who awakens the sleeper; the externality is the solicitous mother who calls one; the externality is the roll call that brings the soldier to his feet; the externality is the reveille that helps one to make the great effort; but the absence of the externality can mean that the inwardness itself calls inwardly to a person. Alas, it can also mean that the inwardness will fail to come.[5]

This so-called externality is the impetus, the pull that we finally stop resisting because of fear, doubt, or anger. It is the manifestation of the hunger in the world, to which we choose to respond, despite the continual need to contend with our own unresolved hunger. It is a step beyond the womb of comfort, assurance, and certainty that we wish to keep around us. It is, as Kierkegaard suggests, a sort of process, an awakening into something new; exactly what, we cannot say. If we could, after all, it wouldn't be faith.

The conundrum for traditional Christianity is that this divests the Church of any authority or power over the veracity of one's individual faith. Faith has as many expressions as there are people and needs in the world, and it can hardly be prescribed by recitation, ritual, or any other symbol we can muster. Even Jesus releases control over the faith of those who are healed. Not only does he point to their own faith as having the power to heal; he sends them out on their own to share such healing with the world.

But how can he do that? He doesn't know exactly what they believe. They haven't had the proper training. They haven't been baptized, memorized Scripture, or signed the membership ledger.

In fact, I think both Kierkegaard and Jesus might agree that the person who makes a claim of faith, and then proceeds to live life as usual, has not actually experienced the leap to faith that truly moves us to meaningful transformation. It is a leap into the darkness, jumping headlong into the unknown, simply because the call to do so is itself sufficient. Faith is never done. Faith is not safe. And faith certainly is not something over which the Church has particular authority.

And yet we have promoted ourselves as the gatekeepers to the world. We are the purveyors, the arbiters of that saving faith. We know how it is achieved, and we determine who is worthy and who is not. We are doing this on behalf of God, of course, but it is a necessary process for quality control.

But Jesus didn't send people to church. He saw the faith bubbling up inside them, pushing them through the crowds, past their doubts, beyond the social stigmas that sought to keep them in their proper place. In some cases, it was the religious leaders who sought to silence them, but still they cried out. Their longing was palpable. It moved him, and he responded.

He acknowledged the faith that drove them, awakened them to its healing, transforming properties, and with one word, set them on a new course:

GO.

A LOVE-HATE RELATIONSHIP WITH LABELS

When everyone believed the world was flat, it was easy to explain what happened when ships went over the horizon: they fell off. When Earth was a plate balanced on the back of enormous turtles, it was easy to explain what was holding up the turtles: more turtles. But if the world is round, that means it must keep going. That also means we have no idea what's out there. And if our planet is an infinitesimal speck, suspended within an endless yet ever-expanding universe...

Well, that's enough to make anyone feel pretty insignificant.

In the middle of a time when nothing seems to have boundaries and everything that was once black and white now falls along a hazy spectrum of gray, there's appeal in holding a kind of contempt for all types of labels. It is this contempt that has led to racism, sexism, and genocide. It is our tendency to stereotype and generalize that has caused so much pain throughout history.

Considering early humans, in prehistoric times, the ability to discriminate was a necessary tool for survival. If a Neanderthal stood around to perform a detailed analysis on whether an animal was a relatively harmless herbivore, appropriate for dinner, or a vicious carnivore, he'd *become* breakfast before he *ate* breakfast. We're born with this innate ability—and need—to put things in their proper place in our minds for future recall. We need to be able to pull on our memories of past objects and experiences quickly so we can think and act quickly. Our level of awareness is so complex and sophisticated that, if we didn't have this ability, we would not be able to function.

Alternatively, rather than viewing labels as overly simplistic, we embrace and enforce them without regard for what may lie beyond. Historically, organized religion has tended to fall more heavily in this camp.

Faith or Certainty?

Adherence to certain doctrines or dogmas, baptism, communion, a blessing from a priest or pastor, approval from organized religion, attendance at a church, or giving a certain amount of money to charity does not make you a Christian. Many people may argue this, but each person has to decide for themselves whether they consider themselves Christian or not, and what that means. Just because someone else—even a person of religious authority—calls another "Christian" or not doesn't necessarily make it so in the heart of that person. Ultimately, to be a passionately committed follower of Jesus is a personal matter of the heart, not of religious doctrine.

Some church leaders will claim that is heresy because it strips them of authority in the process. This is a slippery slope into religious relativism that is a free-for-all, everyone picking and choosing what they like, as if their faith were a grocery store. But assuming there is such a thing as "ultimate, singular Truth" with a capital "T" and there is no such thing as un-interpreted Scripture, then *everyone* does this already at some level.

You may recite the prayers and verses as you have been taught, but no one can *make* you believe anything. It's a choice—that is fundamental to free will.

Why, then, even bother being a Christian? Furthermore,

does the Church have any role at all to play in our life as a follower of Christ?

Rather than building a theology around the idea that "Jesus died for your sins," consider what a theology of "Thy kingdom come" might look like. This phrase, spoken by Jesus, is now known as the Lord's Prayer, and its purpose and goal have been greatly debated. Is it looking forward to a day when the saved shall be gathered together as God's beloved and favored in a heavenly, celestial kingdom, where we will spend the rest of eternity in a state of bliss?

Perhaps. But there's really no way to know what happens for sure after we die. So the problem we're left with is what to do now, today, about "Thy kingdom come." We can conform it into being the kind of leap of faith we take into a sense of safety and certainty that we are taken care of. Or we can take the approach of Kierkegaard's "leap to faith," heeding the command of Jesus to "go" once we are awakened to our own call toward faith.

Social and religious leaders like Martin Luther King Jr. and Walter Rauschenbusch seemed to believe that the line "Thy kingdom come, Thy will be done, on earth as it is in heaven" is an expression of longing for God's love to be fully realized here and now, for our shortcomings and brokenness to be reconciled on this earth, in this life, and not just someday after we die. This is not likely something to which we will entirely arrive in a lifetime, but it is something toward which we should reorient ourselves daily, in order to seek it out, actively and vocally, in all we do. This is Christ's call to the world.

Leap out.

Go.

Be the faith you claim, even as that faith expresses itself only as a deep longing for something not yet present.

In so much as we are all brothers and sisters, all part of a greater body, we cannot be fully made well or whole until all are made well. A faith that claims wholeness and assurance while others are lost or suffering is one based on wishes and desire, rather than actual faith. We wish the hunger would stop. We wish for resolution to our faith, but faith itself is restless, unresolved.

We leap toward it anyway. With our whole selves, not trusting that all will be well and, in making the leap, that we will land finally on firm ground. We leap out because it is the faithful response to an ever-present call.

CHAPTER SEVEN

FROM BREAST TO CROSS

THE CHRISTIAN SCANDAL OF LUST

Historically, the Christian response to lust can be summed up in two words: "bad" and "no." Modern sexual purity movements such as the "Modest is Hottest" campaign come from a place of benevolence, hoping to protect young people from the emotional and even physical damage that can be wreaked through unfettered expressions of lust. But we're at fault when we deny that the lustful urges we all experience are real, inevitable parts of what it means to be human.

Rather than dealing outright with how to manage or express these urges in healthy ways, and to come to terms with them as part of who we are—arguably as a part of what we were made to be—we cordon such desire off, focusing instead only on enforcing the practice of abstinence.

But in severing the lustful inclinations from the rest of our psyches, we actually leave the issue of lust unaddressed. We still lust; we simply can't act on it. Often, shame for even having such lustful feelings or fantasies is added to our self-denial. We experience disembodiment, as our consciousness seeks out ways to express the lust anyway. And when it rears its head, we are overwhelmed with a sense of self-loathing, because we have failed in the eyes of those who have taught us to suppress and abstain. And we're left with a curious contradiction that is difficult to untangle throughout the rest of our lives as Christians:

Sex is dirty; save it for marriage.

There was a time when it was more common to see the naked breast of the nursing Virgin Mary in a sanctuary than a cross. These images, called *Maria Lactans*, depicted an infant Jesus nursing at his mother's breast. This was nothing particularly new, considering that similar themes could be found in artwork dating all the way back to ancient Egypt, which showed the goddess Horus nursing as a symbol of fertility. In the Christian context, particularly during the Dark Ages when so many suffered the effects of starvation and disease, the depictions of Mary offered a sense of God's provision and sustenance.

Around the fifteenth century, these images began to disappear from places of worship, replaced predominantly by crosses. Suddenly the Virgin Mary's naked breast, though offering nourishment for the Messiah, was considered vulgar, leading the minds of the faithful astray in God's house. The images became sexualized, scandalized, dirty. Where previously they were symbols to strengthen people's faith, now they were aiding and abetting our dark slide into sexual sin.

In the broader culture, there were other things that contributed to the problem. First were the advances in medicine and the study of the human body. Before science had really begun to explore our innermost parts, the human body was seen more as a temple in the literal sense, as described in Scripture. It was sacred housing for the soul, mysterious and inexplicable. As we learned how to cut ourselves open and study how all the pieces fit together, the human body was reduced to little more than an assemblage of bloody, though well-assembled, parts in the public's imagination. We were animated meat.

Around this same time, the printing press was invented, enabling the spread of information on a much larger scale. The first book to be printed with the moving typeset technology was a version of the Bible known today as the Gutenberg Bible, which sparked a revolution in the popular consumption of literature and, in particular, the Holy Scriptures. The printing press also fueled the spread of lascivious literature and imagery, which would now be considered early pornography.[1]

Just as it was in the Garden of Eden, we couldn't un-open our eyes once they'd truly been opened. The serpent was loose.

A HISTORY OF SEXUAL SCANDAL

Lust takes many forms, often luring us toward wealth and power, the sirens of worth that culture raises up as the idols of modern society. Though we lust for many things in our lives, such as prestige or material gain, none has affected the institution of the Christian Church, none has left such a profound and ongoing mark, as unchecked sexual desire.

We are all too familiar with the lurid stories that grab the headlines today about priests caught sexually abusing children or married pastors found consorting with male prostitutes. Though it may seem that we're on the crest of a great wave of scandal, this kind of dynamic has been present within the Christian faith for centuries. Consider Augustine of Hippo, one of the most revered saints in the Christian Church, and his admissions to wrestling with similar temptations.

As early as the fourth and fifth centuries, now-sanctified Christian leaders like Augustine confessed the complicated dynamics between their faith and their lustful impulses. One of his most famous prayers from his *Confessions* was for God to "grant me chastity and continence, but not yet."[2] The passionate, secretive relationship of Heloise and Abelard in the early twelfth century shows how even some of the greatest, most influential thinkers in Christian history are, too, beset by scandal. Even as a young woman, Heloise clearly had a brilliant mind, one that required particular tending. Her uncle and caretaker, Fulbert, hired Abelard to be her private tutor. Though he was decades older than she, the two embarked on a torrid romance.

Abelard tried to get Heloise to marry him in secret so that their forbidden love could be reconciled with their mutual Christian faith, but Heloise balked, asserting that choosing a lover was a more powerful bond than marriage, which she argued was really more of a civil contract than a holy sacrament.[3] Abelard persisted, and finally, Heloise agreed to a secret marriage. On learning of the relationship, Fulbert was enraged. He announced the marriage publicly in an effort to protect Heloise's reputation. Then, under the cloak of night, he sent two servants into Abelard's room and had him castrated.[4] Fearing a violent reaction from Fulbert toward Heloise, Abelard had her hidden away in a convent, where she lived under the nuns' protection. Under the patient care and influence of the Sisters, Heloise went on to become a widely renowned writer, theologian, and nun, influential in the formation of modern Christian identity, though the specter of her affair with Abelard followed her wherever she went.

Such scandals are hardly exclusive to Christians. As sexual beings, all of us struggle to channel our desires in healthy, constructive ways. It is a rich and complex part of our collective human history. While recognizing that this is part of the history of the Christian faith, these examples hardly carry the emotional weight for us that contemporary stories do. In the past fourteen years, I have been actively involved in five church communities. Of those, three have had some kind of sexual scandal in their past. In one case, the pastor engaged in a sexual relationship with a congregant. Another pastor was accused of having multiple affairs over several years while also leading the church and raising two children with his wife. He was eventually stripped of his ministerial standing and left ministry entirely. Still a third senior pastor was arrested for stealing money from his own church, and spending it on, among other things, drugs and strippers.

It is enough to dishearten and discourage even the most faithful among us, and yet there are those rare occasions when we see the subtle work of the Divine, even in the middle of such profound human brokenness.

REVEREND DAVE, THE SEX ADDICT

I contributed to a book a couple of years ago about young adult sexuality and faith called *Oh God, Oh God, Oh God!*

Aside from being quite possibly the most awesome book title ever, the subject matter itself was important, and one around which the Church far too often falls short. I took part in a workshop about the book, and afterward a male pastor, who I'll call "Dave," came up to talk to me.

"Thank you for giving us all permission to talk about this," he said. "This may be the first time I've heard people in ministry actually talk openly about sex and sexuality in a faith context, short of the same old 'just say no' rhetoric." He went on to explain that he had struggled for many years with sexual addiction, and that one of the biggest problems he experienced was that there was no one he could talk to about his struggle. So in a moment of brazen journalistic inspiration, I asked him if I could interview him about his struggle for this book. The quotations that follow are pulled verbatim from his written responses to my questions.

"I got to my first twelve-step group" for sex addiction, he said, "and four of the fifteen guys in attendance were clergy. But no one wants to talk about this." He went on to explain the group perceived that the two most common professions entering into sex-related recovery groups were pilots and clergy.

There are established, common criteria for a job that tends either to harbor or even cultivate sexual addicts within its ranks. The three most common factors in those jobs are:

- A position that involves a high degree of public exposure (not *that* kind of exposure, but rather some significant amount of public visibility);
- A high level of monotony or boredom, and;

- A greater than average amount of power, often largely unchecked on a day-to-day basis.[5]

"I had a great amount of time on my hands," he said. "Clergy do visit people, but in a small to medium-sized congregation, regular visiting may not be helpful for the congregation or clergy. Some people rehearse the same litanies of problems, concerns, and joys. So there is this wad of time that many pastors have."

Dave's greatest struggle was helping those within his congregation who were wrestling with the same kinds of issues from which he was trying to escape. "I could not find a place to relax and get away," he said. His problems, and those of others, followed him everywhere. He considered temporary escape at the gym or golf course, but such leisure activities evoked too much guilt. "But," said Dave, "I could go home and say I was working."

Unfortunately, Dave's description of the church he served is characteristic of the typical mainline Protestant church these days: small to medium sized, resistant to change, content to churn through the same traditions, habits, and problems that have been around for decades. As such, the leaders and clergy lose heart and tire of the struggle, succumbing to the numbing boredom of empty ritual, while also depending on their paycheck—however meager—to keep the bills paid.

Combine that kind of soul-numbing routine with constant stress about your church's decline, a high degree of public exposure, and unchecked power, and you've just described the typical twenty-first-century Western world minister.

"I had to be more heroic in my fake persona," says Dave, "to compensate for the fact that I was addicted to pornography. There was lots of shame about it. That shame made me feel awful because I would talk about Jesus loving every person...except me.

"How do I numb the pain of shame? Porn and masturbation. What is at the root of more shame? Porn and masturbation. It is hell."

Dave shared a story with me about a mom whose twelve-year-old son was in jail for molesting his younger stepsister. Apparently the parents left the girl with their near-teenage son, who then ordered the girl to perform oral sex on him. The father of the boy had pornography all around the house and on the television, but he had dealt with this by telling his son not to look at it. This, of course, worked about as well as any reasonable person might expect. The young boy was exposed to a variety of imagery that he, in his young emotional state, had no capacity to process on his own, and yet he felt shame for having disobeyed his father's rules.

This deeply rooted shame joined with the fertile soil of a sexually hypercharged preteen boy, an unsupervised home environment, and time to kill, and well, you can imagine how one thing led to another.

"I sat in the room listening," says Dave, "not judging, knowing exactly what happened and how he got there. I had never been there, but I understood completely." Of course he did. The boy's situation was not unlike his own.

"I went to visit the kid almost every week in jail," he says. "In September of that year, I finally decided that I had nothing to offer him unless I got myself together." Dave bought a copy of Patrick Carnes's book *Hope and Recovery*, and read it in two hours. As soon as he read the last word, he fell to his knees and begged Jesus to take the addiction away: a prayer he says was answered. He went to his first twelve-step meeting and started a program of recovery that he has been practicing ever since.

"I learned more about discipleship in those twelve-step meetings," says Dave, "than I ever did in seminary."

FILLING THE DREADED GAP

The first tenet of Buddhism, central to all of its teaching, is that "Life is suffering." For some, this is a terrifying prospect. It is nothing but bad news. Suffering, it seems, is something to be avoided. Why would we invite suffering if we had any alternative?

But that's not the point. The statement is a call for clarity, for acceptance of things the way they are, for all people to embrace the fact that life does include, at its heart, a fair share (or unfair share, depending on how you look at it) of suffering. The experience of suffering isn't in itself a by-product of sin. It's not some punishment doled out by God for wrongdoing, some giant karmic payback. It is a natural by-product of being human, and of the separation we experience from our Creator. But it is related very closely to sin, particularly when we seek to find the loophole, the shortcut around the dark valley of suffering.

When we seek to avoid suffering, we end up spreading it around. We leave a trail of it behind us as we run from it, like carrying a giant bag of poison with a hole in the bottom. If we keep moving, the poison may never pile up and consume us, but we can do a hell of a lot of damage by pouring the toxic waste out on everyone else we come into contact with.

That is sin.

Desire in and of itself is not at the heart of the sin of lust. It's when we follow those desires as a means to find a shortcut around our suffering that it mutates into something worse. If we sit with the sense of lack, we can come to terms with the emptiness. We have to resist the temptation to satisfy this desire, once and for all, though such emptiness seems infinite, all-consuming, too powerful to face. And as such, we run from emptiness or stuff it down, bartering our own lives, our peace, and that of others around us as collateral damage. The pursuit of desire grows like a consuming flame that will devour everything in its path. It metastasizes into an addiction that we worship, to which we are beholden. It is the idol that takes the place of God in our lives.

For Dave, sex was his tool of choice for trying to avoid the suffering experienced in unfulfilled desire. The good news is that Dave finally chose to face the emptiness, the un-fill-able void, seeking God's strength and the compassion of his brothers and sisters in recovery to help him through that Valley of the Shadow of Death. Far too many end up staying in the valley, however, convinced there is no way out or, worse, that they have brought this fate upon themselves and that they somehow deserve it.

The beautiful irony of the valley is that we emerge on the other side, reborn, into something new, something more wonderful than we could have imagined in our brokenness. But in trying to find another way around the valley, in trying to avoid the very thing we fear the most, we're allowing our lives to be consumed by an utterly pointless task. We're not really living.

"I'm not a writer," Dave told me, "but I have this experience, and Jesus has called me to be useful. Not great, but useful. I really see my disease as the greatest gift God could have given me." At first, I was shocked by this idea that a sexual addiction could be seen as a gift from God. But as I sat with it for a while, it began to make more sense.

It wasn't that Dave was saying God made him a sex addict, or that he had been put through this on purpose, so that he could minister to other people dealing with similar issues. What he meant was that, once he was willing to set his own ego and shame aside, to admit he was powerless without God's help to overcome this problem, God began moving in unexpectedly beautiful ways. Not only did God and Dave conspire to piece a broken life back together, but Dave came out on the other side of the experience with the tools necessary to help other people do the same thing.

God uses brokenness to make something new, something even stronger or more beautiful out of the pieces, not in spite of the brokenness, but because of it. Of course, if God could do this with Jesus' brokenness, maybe we shouldn't be so surprised when it happens to the rest of us.

NOW WHAT?

In many cases, the Church has failed to provide people with the tools to live as fully embodied children of God. Instead, we're taught to be ashamed of our bodies and encouraged to cover them and not talk about physical things in case such thoughts lead us down the slippery path of sin. Meanwhile, stories bubble up in the media about priests and ministers abusing their positions of power, exploiting women, children, or even other men sexually. Not surprisingly, this combination of problems has led many to walk away from religion, labeling it as irrelevant at best, or brazenly hypocritical at worst.

Clearly the Church can learn much from those within and beyond its walls who commit themselves to healing the sexual brokenness of others that comes from addiction or abuse. But first, we must give ourselves permission to speak openly about such uncomfortable subjects, and also admit our own struggles and fears around such issues.

Since the Church is so lost on matters of sex and sexuality, a case could be made that it shouldn't be involved in such conversations at all. But aside from the biological necessities and physical recreation related to sexuality, it is a gift of the Spirit. It is a means by which we express ourselves to one another and by which we bond more intimately than in any other way. Though it is powerful, complex, and can be dangerous when mishandled, sexuality is indeed a gift from God. It's not as if God is sitting up in Heaven looking down and thinking, "Whoa, what are they doing to each other now?"

Rather than seeking to provide definitive answers, our faith communities should be creating the safe spaces where we can ask the difficult questions, admit our struggles, and hold one another up in loving support and accountability when we fall short. Of course, this safety is predicated on the assumption that our vulnerability will not be preyed upon when we take the risks. This requires an equal measure of humble confession and transparency from everyone involved. Without that assurance, and until we have gone to every effort to mend the damage already done, we have no legitimate place at the table.

Like Dave, we're broken. But God can use even this if we lay our shortcomings bare beneath the light of humble confession. We can't undo the hurt that has already been done, but as in the Catholic tradition, we can admit our wrongs, demonstrate contrition, and do what we can to be different from today forward. We can't reclaim any of our lives already lost to desire, but we can resolve to live fully by breaking our addiction to the lust that takes so much from us, if we allow it.

Chapter Eight

Re-Membering

The Christ-like Virtue of Love

Love gives meaning to life. It is used synonymously with the nature and name of God. But it requires a lot from us: all of us, in fact. It stakes a claim on our souls, once we surrender to it. But with that surrender comes a terrifying sense of vulnerability.

Following the birth of our son, Mattias, Amy preached about this kind of soul-wrenching love:

The most humbling experience in my life—by far—was becoming a mother. I gave up a lot of control the day Mattias was born. I didn't have a choice. He was his own person. He was in the world, no longer in me.

The moment they picked him up and showed him to me a piece of me became him. Immediately, so much love—so much life. Later that night he and I sat alone in our hospital room. I held him and cried.

"You didn't tell me that it was going to be like this, God. He's the most amazing, most beautiful thing I've ever seen, but he's not mine. Oh sure, now he's content—he doesn't know what sort of world

he's just come into, or how frightening and dangerous it can be.

"Sure, hopefully he will grow up and get to experience many of life's splendors and learn for himself of the
beauty and wisdom in this world, but he's also going
to get hurt. People are mean. He's going to get picked
on. He's going to be wrong. He's going to break his
arm. He's going to get lost. He's going to get his heart
broken—no. No, he can't.

He can't have his heart broken because that's my
heart. You didn't tell me that he would take my heart,
God. If anyone should know, you should, God. You
should know what it's like to have a son. You should
know what it's like to be so vulnerable."

And then I said it, "This isn't fair."

In religious circles, we're more than willing to speak of the
goodness of God, and we even look to Scripture to support our
radical claim that "God is Love." And then we go out into the
world and experience this love, and it's not always good. Love,
after all, is terrifying, risky, and fraught with danger.

A mother gives birth to a child who later dies, taking much
of her heart with him. A spouse pours himself into his wife,
only to be betrayed, left with the scars that barely hold together the gaping wound that once was his heart. Amy is
right; love isn't fair. In fact, sometimes it really sucks. And yet
we continue to proclaim that God is this love, while on the
other hand, confessing the same God's everlasting goodness
and justice. But if we understand God to be perfectly good,
and if we can agree that Love is not always good, then we
need to bridge the chasm between these two ideas.

Such questions, left unattended, are fertile ground for the bitterness, hurt, and doubt that drive so many from the communities preaching of a love that no one actually seems to possess, at least not for long, and certainly not without consequence. We begin to peek beyond the rainbows and felt-board characters of the story of Noah's ark, only to find an angry, violent God. Is this love?

We leap to Easter Sunday, often turning a willfully blind eye to the bloodiness and brokenness of Good Friday, the day that paints a picture of a God who sets up Jesus for a humiliating, undeserved death. How in the world can this be love? And so we lose hope, lose heart, lose faith in the God of our Sunday school classes. They become flimsy façades, behind which lurks the truth, and about which no one dares to speak.

Yes, love is a risk. Yes, the Bible presents many faces of an often-confounding God. But instead of dwelling on whether or not love—and therefore, God—is purely and eternally good, maybe we should be asking ourselves a very different question:

Is love worth it?

THE LETHAL LOVE OF *BREAKING BAD*

Walt is a high school chemistry teacher who finds out he has late-stage lung cancer, and the only treatment available with any promise isn't covered by his insurance. He decides he needs some quick money both to cover the treatments and to provide for his family in his anticipated absence. So what better to do than to join forces with a former dope-head student and start cooking up the finest crystal meth?

Walt devolves from a simple teacher and family man into a hardened drug kingpin, all under the pretense of providing for those whom he loves. And although he justifies his illegal pursuits because of this love, it's the very thing that threatens to destroy him, his family, their home, and everything else he cares about.

It seems that love can be terribly destructive. No one can argue that Walt doesn't love his family, and if he didn't have them to care for, it's clear in the story that he would have foregone the expensive treatment and let nature take its course. But love appears to be the only culprit. Granted, Walt made a series of compromising choices along the way, and there are loads of justifications in his wake, but without the love for his family, none of this would have happened.

If this is really love, then the human heart should be categorized as a concealed weapon. The mind may hatch the schemes and formulate the justifications, the hands may build the bombs and wield the swords, but the heart, driven supposedly by love, is the match to the fuse that sets the whole damned thing in motion.

Even Scripture was aware of these wildly powerful, often hard to tame, properties of love. In the book of 1 Timothy, Paul offers a grave warning about love. Though the well-known quote is often believed to say, "Money is the root of all evil," the actual quote is, "For the love of money is the root of all evil.[*]" Jesus, too, knew that money is a big stumbling block for us even in his day, given that he refers to money more times than anything else in the Gospels.

But we tend to get hung up on the money part and miss

---

[*] 1 Timothy, 6:10

the real point. We could take out the word "money" and replace it with any number of things (sex, drugs, power, ego) and the effect is still the same. So at the core of the warning from the prophet, echoed as well throughout Jesus' ministry, is a shocking and unsettling proposal:

Can love, *when misdirected or misapplied, be the root of all evil?* If we invest our love in anything other than God first, it mutates into idolatry, making room for no other. It is a selfish, consuming, jealous kind of love, and yet one that never satisfies.

We don't like hearing this. We prefer to focus on love as white doves, big hugs, smiling children, and olive branches. Or we like to talk about Jesus' sacrificial love for us. But that's still not a complete picture. Consider the image that Timothy is painting. The prophet isn't saying that love itself is evil; he's saying that it is the taproot, the means by which evil gains its nourishment. A root system, after all, doesn't discriminate between pure water and a poisoned source when it is passing through. Love is, by definition, a wide-open gate, though which all may pass, sometimes for better or worse.

We have some choices, then, when tapping into this root source of love. We can enjoy the benefits, bathing in the wild grace and holy bonds that are fruits of such a source, while ignoring the risks involved. We can also justify the evil as inevitable, shrugging our shoulders, or even arguing that the love makes the collateral damage all worth it. Or we can cut the root off at the base, severing ourselves from love, in order to mitigate the risk of the dangers that accompany it.

Where do the toxins that taint the so-called well come from? Look in the mirror. The potential is always there, because love is powerful, and where there is power, there is always the potential for evil in the hands of humanity. Our shadow sides grasp for such power, with designs on achieving less than noble means. How, after all, can it be a bad thing if the source is love?

All Christians, and particularly Christian ministers, speak often of God's love. But occasionally, the subject is given a far more superficial treatment than it deserves. Or maybe a more appropriate description is that we sometimes present an immature description of love and, therefore, an immature understanding of God.

We pray to this God for fulfillment of our wishes. God is hardly more than Santa Claus within this particular theology, with us climbing onto God's lap to make our request and then waiting until the day when our order will be filled. This, much like an infant's understanding of love, is entirely selfish and immature and encourages the self-focused kind of Christianity that supports the notion some outside of the faith have that many of us are merely greedy narcissists, cloaked in the righteousness of our religion to justify it.

We also offer a "good feeling God," the one that is the subject of so many praise and worship songs, the one that makes our teeth white, brightens our smiles, and fills our hearts with song, day in and day out. But then the time inevitably comes when the good feeling fades and we're left wanting (feelings which we were promised this God would drive out, once and for all). So we're left with two choices: go back to the source of this feeling we long to hang on to (i.e., the Church), or come to terms with the fact that we, unlike our Christian brothers and sisters, seem to be undeserving of the adolescent kind of love presented by the faith we claim.

To be fair, these false representations of God or love are purveyed throughout mainstream culture as well. Indeed, our entire capitalist economy depends on the pretense that the hunger we struggle with can be fixed, and that any particular product or service making the claim might, finally, be the one to bring the sense of wholeness and contentment which we all long for. But while it is understandable that the Church would absorb these cultural values, we are charged as followers of the Way of Jesus to demand more. Not more for ourselves in the sense that we tend to think of it, but rather more from love. More from God and *more from ourselves*.

Our understanding of love evolves throughout our lifetimes. To an infant, love is a mother's breast, a soothing voice, and a warm, comforting embrace. As we grow, the rules of love become increasingly transactional. We are expected to demonstrate our love through acts of kindness, generosity, and deference. As adults, we seek partnership, someone to bear witness to our lives, and someone for whom we can do the same. A fuller, more mature love like this is based in covenant. And covenant, by its very nature, requires parity, equal investments on both sides. Therefore, if we place our love into things such as money, power, sex, organized religion, or even false constructs of God that bend only to serve our whims, there is no reciprocity involved. But real love requires that *everything* be placed second, including our own desires, our agendas, our need for control, our expectations, our well-founded fears that with such love comes great risk. But it is what is required of us. *All of us.*

It's hard to imagine how such love might manifest itself in the world, what might happen if such power passed through humanity into the company of creation. It would take someone entirely human to express that love in terms we could understand, yet also completely transcendent of the humanity that taints the source. A convergence of God and creation in a space that would likely change the course of history forever.

Imagine what we would do if we witnessed such perfect love. We might fall to our knees in awe, drop everything to follow wherever it might lead. Or we might spit on it, place it high on a cross, and hang it by nails out of anger and jealousy. We would pierce its sides, fearful that such a love would cause the very foundations we've built for ourselves to crumble. We would kill it, hoping somehow that, with its final breaths, such a perfect love would die with it, while also holding out hope in our heart of hearts that the promise of such an indomitable love really was true. We want to believe it, though it scares us at the same time. We want to submit ourselves to it, but with the guarantee that everything will end well. We want the reward without the risk, though love requires that we take the risk first, without any promise of reward.

We love for the sake of love itself. We love because it's the stuff from which we're made. We can choose to deny it, but in doing so, we're denying the most basic part of our nature.

CRAZY LOVE

The kind of love we're called to by Jesus is insane. In human terms of self-preservation, it makes no sense. We surrender all control, make ourselves vulnerable to those who seek to destroy us, submit to an authority greater than ourselves. It's against our human nature. It defies logic. And we know, as history shows, what the world tends to do when confronted with such truth.

It's also a little maddening to realize that we'll never entirely "get there" in this lifetime. This love is something to be experienced and to strive for, but never to possess as our own. Love is transcendent, and I'm not, but there's a part of me that, despite the hurt, the disappointment, and most of all the fear, holds me back, keeps me turning back toward this love.

Amy got an e-mail from a fellow pastor who was reeling after a recent event at her church, which she describes as holding more socially and theologically conservative positions than her and her husband. Following was part of what she wrote:

> My husband and I are at XYZ church where I am the Family Minister, and we started a new emergent and progressive worship gathering last November (we are open and affirming in the emergent service, but not in our regular service). I consider myself a progressive Christian, lovin' me some Peter Rollins, Marcus Borg and John Shelby Spong to name a few. Yet, I am in a congregation that has some fairly conservative members…ironically most of whom happen to be near my age (young thirties).
>
> We brought Peter Rollins to town this summer, and that has ruffled the feathers of a few of the more conservative members. They are engaging our pastor and me in conversation about the authority of scripture and "how can Peter call himself a Christian if he doesn't care if someone ultimately chooses God?" Actually

what Peter said at the lunch with these two members was "I don't necessarily care about 'what' someone believes...I'm more interested in how they believe." Pretty freakin' genius if you ask me, but not what these gals wanted to hear.

I am struggling with how to minister at this church all the while being my progressive self...who aims to gather our people around a common language and maintain our diverse community. How do you and Christian experience your ministry among diverse congregants in your community? I am feeling pretty defeated right now...that ultimately the conservatives will wind up bailing on us, or that I might have to move on as the "liberal minister." One thing I cannot do is compromise who I am. I have walked a long and hard road away from conservative Christianity to get to the place I am, where I value what I value. And, I can't turn back. I don't mind someone else believing differently, but it makes me really angry when someone says I have to believe like them.

I am not sure there is much encouragement you can say. You and Christian just came to mind as I navigate my way through this difficult impasse of ministry.

Amy offered a response that I think encapsulates some of the essence of what following this path toward love, laid out by Christ, looks like in daily life:

There is an angry and reactionary liberal inside me that wants to fight and scream and blame. But, I know that ultimately that will get me nowhere.

So, I try to focus on the things we can usually agree on—Jesus. We love him, we try to follow him, hope to honor him with our lives. That is where I try to keep the conversation. If this is what we believe, then how can we live this together? What does that look like?

For me, it means sitting next to people in church who I can't stand, whose ideas I can't wrap my heart and mind around, but who God loves. And, I call other people to do the same. We have to hold one another accountable to this standard, lovingly.

So—we all have "that person"—the jerk who insists that God is a "he," the woman who tries to steal pens from the office (when all she'd have to do is ask and we'd give her some), the needy guy who always wants your attention and complains but never changes, the manipulator who starts rumors, the bitch who thinks her kids can do no wrong, yes even her. Ugh—fucking church. It wears me out. And, it is so beautiful when we get over ourselves and love and serve God together. Sorry, but it makes me cuss.

So hold yourself to it and then call others out to do the same. If we REALLY worship the God that Jesus shows us, this is our highest call.

Authentic witness does not deny these differences. It loves beyond them, in full awareness of them, and it tries to free others up to do the same.

I can say that even though our church is not an open and affirming congregation, it was a lesbian couple who wrote that statement of belief and joined the church together a couple of weeks ago. Everyone knows they are lesbians, but because it's Ann and Lisa (names changed), it's okay—we love and trust them. Real, transformative change happens through relationship.

So, sister, love them into the church God has given you the vision to help them become. Authentically. You be the most loving, real, honest "you" that you can be and God will do the rest. I know that is very big and I struggle every day to do the same, but I also know that it is true.

This is part of the strange irony of ministry sometimes, and not just in the professional clergy sense. It's the irony of trying to live out the message of this crazy love as we understand it in a world that is scared nearly to death by it. We long to share a love we can't entirely express, but only sometimes point toward. The path to this love is beset on all sides by these shadow-selves of our own making, intent on using the same love we claim as a wedge to drive us farther apart.

Even Jesus struggled with the open-ended nature of such a love sometimes. Consider again the story of the Canaanite woman who sought a blessing of healing from Jesus. His response: he called her a dog and dismissed her request, at least at first. The Jews and the Canaanites had a history, not unlike the kind of struggle we see between many Christians and Muslims today. Think of the encounter as sort of like how many people reacted to the construction of a mosque near Ground Zero in New York. I'd like to think I would look past the ideologies and differences to the human being at the heart of the request, but I'm not so sure I'd have been able to.

Sure, some folks prefer to frame Jesus' rebuke of the woman as a test of faith, but as I've said, I understand it as a glimpse of his own human, shadow side. He was, after all, entirely human, as we understand him, while also being divine. So if he was utterly human, he must have experienced the same struggles of other-ness and the shadow sides of love with which we wrestle every day.

It is this darker dimension of love that serves to divide, to dismember us as part of a greater body, to shred us limb from limb, scattering us like ashes across a soulless landscape. And yes, even ministers do it. We cling to what we believe is right so fervently that all others who might resist or oppose the Gospel as we understand it must be pushed aside, dealt with, pressed into conformity, or else. This human tendency knows no political party, religion, or social agenda. We all share this like a cancer we'd all just as soon pretend doesn't exist. But as soon as we do, it spreads, takes on its own will, fed by our willful ignorance. And as such, we are agents of the destruction we claim to stand against, all in the name of Love.

In *The Book of Awakening*, author Mark Nepo offers a beautiful picture of what is required of us in living into this more perfect love:

> When young, it was my first fall from love. It broke me open the way lightning splits a tree. Then, years later, cancer broke me further. This time, it broke me wider, the way a flood carves the banks of a narrow stream. Then, having to leave a twenty-year marriage. This broke me the way wind shatters glass. Then, in Africa, it was the anonymous face of a schoolboy beginning his life. This broke me yet again. But this was like hot water melting soap.
>
> Each time, I tried to close up what had been opened.

It was a reflex, natural enough. But the lesson was, of course, the other way. The lesson was in never closing again.[1]

Real love breaks us open. Nepo gets at the heart of the matter, which is that this broken-openness is not a problem to be solved or a disease to be cured with prayer, shopping, sex, or any other self-serving salvific reflex. The call is to live into the brokenness, coming to terms with the impulse we have to try to make it better, to get back to how things were—or at least seemed to be—in the past.

In doing so, we allow ourselves to be remade into something new, fragments of one another joined together along the rough edges of our brokenness, slowly crafted into the face of God, into which our egos dissolve, overcome by the harmony of shared re-creation. We become coconspirators in a most sacred act of re-membering.

At the Communion table, we talk about remembering. Most people think of this as a command from Jesus to keep him in mind, to think back to who he was and what he said and did. But maybe he really meant to re-member him in the world today, every time we come together. If so, it's our job to take his brokenness, our brokenness, and the world's brokenness and try to find a way to make something whole out of it all.

God's kingdom isn't some far-off place being prepared by some invisible sky wizard we call "God," rather it is something only fully realized when we conspire with love to place it first, to allow it to be the thing that holds the world and us together. The thing we are waiting for is ourselves.

Is this love worth it? The answer depends on our own expectations. If we cling to the immature notions of God that we continue to try to tame in our service, such love is unnecessarily dangerous, counterintuitive, even evil.

But if we can get beyond ourselves and join in the collective imagination of something more whole than the sum total of our brokenness, there is nothing other than this love that can ultimately make life worthwhile.

CHAPTER NINE

A GAMBLER'S EMPIRE

THE CHRISTIAN SCANDAL OF GREED

I n the late 1940s a handsome, personable thirtysomething pastor named Oral Roberts sat down to read his Bible, asking God to guide him to the particular Scripture he needed to receive that day. The pages flipped open to the third of three letters, or epistles, and his eyes immediately were drawn to the second verse in his King James Bible:

> *Beloved, I wish above all things that thou mayest prosper and be in health. Even as thy soul prospereth.*[1]

From this, Roberts developed what became known as his "seed faith" philosophy, which posits that, given only a small seedlike gesture of faith (such as a donation to Roberts's ministry), God would multiply it in abundance. He became a multimillionaire as a result.

Today, a study by the Pew Research Center found that nearly three quarters of the Latinos in the United States who identify as having some religious affiliation agreed with the statement "God will grant financial success to all believers who have enough faith,"[2] and claim to identify with what is now known as prosperity gospel. Though this strain of Christianity initially took hold in predominantly low-income Latino and African-American communities, it has since found purchase with a growing number of middle class Americans,[3] as well as in Anglo-dominant suburbs and more affluent urban centers.[4] In a 2009 *Atlantic* article, Hanna Rosin notes that three of the twelve largest churches in America are prosperity gospel churches, and among the 260 biggest congregations in the country, 50 are prosperity gospel churches.[5] In order to understand how such a uniquely American phenomenon came about, it's helpful to consider a bit of broader American cultural history.

In his book *Something for Nothing*, author Jackson Lears considers how the United States' unique combination of political and economic culture, combined with a modern Protestant Christian ethic, could give rise to something like prosperity gospel. In fact, he makes his case so compellingly that it's almost as if the homegrown theological phenomenon was all but inevitable.

Lears delineates two ways of thinking in the United States: there's the *gambler* and the *self-made man*:

One narrative puts the big gamble at the center of American life: from the earliest English settlements at Jamestown and Massachusetts Bay, risky ventures in real estate (and other less palpable commodities) power the progress of a fluid, mobile democracy...The other narrative exalts a different sort of hero—a disciplined self-made man, whose success comes through careful cultivation of (implicitly Protestant) virtues in cooperation with a Providential plan. The first account implies a contingent universe where luck matters and admits that net worth may have nothing to do with moral worth. The second assumes a coherent universe where earthly rewards match ethical merits and suggests that Providence has ordered this world as well as the next.[6]

Most people, given the choice, would choose to identify more with the *self-made man*, and as Lears later points out, it is the personality type held in higher regard in our culture. For example, consider how we think about the person who won his millions playing the lottery versus someone who came from modest means and, through hard work and determination, made their own fortune.

But in every self-made man, there's a little bit of a gambler, too. In fact, I'd argue that each of us bears some admixture of the two. We all want to believe we've earned some of the fortune we have in our lives, and given the research, a healthy cross section of us would also ascribe to a way of thinking that suggests God rewards good, honest, hard work. But if we're part of the archetypal modern American fabric, we're also gamblers.

If you have any money invested in the stock market, you're a gambler. And according to a report issued by the Federal Reserve Board and Bureau of Economic Analysis, the average American household's debt payments in 1945 commanded only about 17 percent of their disposable income. Fast-forward sixty or so years to 2006, and that same debt-to-income balloons 750 percent to more than 120 percent of our disposable income.[7]

Then along came home mortgages, which really took off after the World Wars, when the economy was growing and there was no sense that forward progress would subside in the foreseeable future. Families might take out five- or ten-year notes to get into that home of their dreams that prior generations either would have to inherit or save for decades to afford. When the price of a home started to exceed what could be reasonably paid back in a decade, lenders just stretched out the terms to fifteen, twenty, and then thirty years. When the credit market for those kinds of loans got saturated, up popped the subprime lending market, offering lines of credit to corpses, household pets, and millions of others who had no possible means to pay back what they borrowed.

And now that the bubble has burst, we stand around with our hands in the air, wondering what happened. People from my great-grandparents' generation not only would have seen borrowing money for a car or even a house as stupid; they would have seen it as a moral shortcoming. For those who are more religiously inclined, such indebtedness would have been a sin. They took very seriously the bit in Proverbs that says, "A rich person rules poor people, and a *borrower is a slave to a lender.*"

Outward displays of affluence were bad enough; to borrow money to live beyond your means was practically unimaginable. Some believe that Christianity—and more specifically, prosperity gospel—is at least partly to blame for the financial crisis that boiled over in 2008.

In her article titled "Did Christianity Cause the Crash?" Hanna Rosin draws a correlation between the places in the United States where prosperity gospel is strongest and where subprime lending was most prevalent. She notes that, because of the "hyper-segregated" communities where both tended to be most often found, African-Americans and Latinos were targeted far more than whites.[8]

In many smaller congregations, pastors who can't muster a full-time salary from their ministry seek extra work to make ends meet. And as Rosin discovered, "One theme emerging in these suits (against banks for illegal subprime lending) is how banks teamed up with pastors to win over new customers for subprime loans."[9]

The partnership made for an expedient, if suspicious, marriage of convenience:

The branch managers figured pastors had a lot of influence with their parishioners and could give the loan officers credibility and new customers. [Mortgage lending officer] Jacobson remembers a conference call where sales managers discussed the new strategy. The plan was to send officers to guest-speak at church-sponsored "wealth-building seminars"...and dazzle the participants with the possibility of a new house. They would tell pastors that for every person who took out a mortgage, $350 would be donated to the church, or to a charity of the parishioner's choice. "They wouldn't say, 'Hey, Mr. Minister. We want to give your people a bunch of subprime loans,'" Jacobson told me. "They would say, 'Your congregants will be homeowners! They will be able to live the American dream!'"

When Hanna Rosin asked a pastor at the center of her article how one is to know if the impulse to buy a house is a call from God or old-fashioned greed, she says he answered much like she would expect a roulette dealer to respond. "'Ten Christians will say that God told them to buy a house,' says the pastor. 'In nine of the cases, it will go bad. The tenth one is the real Christian.'" As for the nine for whom it doesn't work out as well, he offers a gambler's consolation. "'For them, there's always another house.'"[10]

In her book, *Blessed: A History of the American Prosperity Gospel*, Kate Bowler distinguishes such apparent transactional types of prosperity teaching as *hard prosperity*. "Hard prosperity emphasized its contractual nature," she writes, "describing God as unable to 'multiply back' blessings except to those who give correctly." She notes that ministries focusing on ideas such as the "hundredfold blessing" based on Mark 10:30 ("*...he will receive a hundred times as much now in the present age, houses and brothers and sisters and mothers and children and farms...*") proliferated particularly in the 1970s when consumer credit was loosened and people came to have an emboldened faith in what she calls an "invisible economy."[11]

Some congregations and pastors even have become entangled in Ponzi schemes, like Pastor Eddie Long's New Birth Missionary Baptist Church, which, in 2012, was investigated (among other pastors and churches) by the SEC for alleged involvement in an $11 million pyramid scheme, which the SEC charged was promoted by another minister, Ephren Taylor, as a financial empowerment seminar. One of the ads for his seminars states, "Will you continue to stand by and let your church drown financially? It's time to take action now by hosting a financial empowerment seminar at (YOUR CONGREGATION) with Minister Ephren W. Taylor, II. Call (877) XXX-1463 as dates are filling fast."[12]

According to a report offered by the *Christian Post*, "Taylor was targeting primarily church congregations, preying on their beliefs and emphasizing their common Christian heritage, appealing to their faith and convincing them that a portion of invested money would be spent on charitable causes and useful community projects, SEC believes. In fact, the money went into a grand pyramid scheme, as well as Taylor's personal usage, the agency alleges."[13]

Collusion between the Church and outside bodies for material gain is hardly a unique by-product of modern Western life. In fact, we can credit the predominance of Christianity worldwide in large part to a similar partnership.

A CHRISTIAN EMPIRE

There are few—if any—better examples throughout history of systemic institutional greed than those found in the marriage of the Roman Empire to the Christian Church, some sixteen hundred years ago. At the time, the Church was consistently under threat by the government because they, themselves, operated independent of Roman rule. Christianity was still a relatively small but growing faith, and Roman leadership saw this as potentially problematic. But in this threat also was an opportunity: a marriage of convenience by which both the Church and the Roman Empire could expand their reach and influence, while also amassing unprecedented wealth. This, in short, was the birth of Christendom.

"Christendom" is one of those nerdy Christian words that sometimes gets mistaken as a synonym for "Christianity" as a whole. But it's actually very different, and the difference is important. Culturally, the word is sometimes used in reference to the faith, but in a political context, the word points to the phenomenon of Christianity being the dominant voice in the moral fabric and cultural dialogue of a nation. It is fundamental to the root identity of a national culture, and as such, it holds tremendous sway in guiding the direction of the culture.

That is, at least until those roots begin to atrophy or they come under attack from an outside force powerful enough to liberate the culture from the grasp of the religion.

I know this sounds like Christendom is a bad thing, and history suggests it generally is. It is true that the Christian faith informed parts of the Constitution of the United States and our original democratic form of government. However, many of the values people often attribute to Christianity can also be found in other religions or cultures. It's just when Christianity is no longer the assumed norm of the land that such claims about us being a Christian nation begin to create a sense of dissonance within the larger cultural identity and conversation. The tendency of Christendom, when challenged, is to impose itself by force. And although we do not have a nationally mandated religion, there are more subtle ways in which people can be made to feel inferior or on the outside of the social norm if they do not ascribe to the Christian identity presented to them.

"Christendom" operates much like how we think of bullies on the playground. After all, you don't walk up and start picking a fight with the bully on the first day of school, right? Sure, he may be nice most of the time, and he may even offer "protection" to some of the punier kids. But the fact remains that he came into his power either by force or the threat of force, and he stays there because of the fear others have toward him.

The word often used to describe this sort of dominance is "hegemony," which means one group holds effective dominance over all others in a given area, country, or part of the world. In the West, in recent centuries, Christianity could be said to have enjoyed a sort of hegemonic presence on a multinational scale, for many of the same self-serving reasons that it was embraced by the powers that be in the fourth century.

But that's changing.

Such a powerful and long-standing church-state partnership is a tough one to dissolve, but the ground has been shifting beneath our feet in the West for the past several decades. There was a time when having a Catholic run for President was shocking; in 2012, there was only one Protestant Christian among the four presidential and vice-presidential candidates in the race. It's no longer social or professional suicide to admit openly a disbelief in God or not to attend one's local church.

As noted by a study conducted by the Pew Forum, "...the number of people who say they are unaffiliated with any particular faith today (16.1 percent) is more than double the number who say they were not affiliated with any particular religion as children. Among Americans ages 18–29, one-in-four say they are not currently affiliated with any particular religion."[14]

And as people drift away from organized religion by the millions, its influence over the culture diminishes. As such, it loses clout within the political sphere (which arguably has suffered its own share of credibility crises in recent generations). People seem to be losing faith in institutions in general, both to serve their individual interests and to dictate what "normal" will be for our culture.

That, barring an act of God, is the beginning of the end of Christendom in the West. And for those truly seeking the way of Jesus, this can be a good thing. For one, it is an opportunity for us as a religion to atone for the greed and resulting oppression and violence done in God's name. Much of the material wealth and power the Church has enjoyed was gained through unsavory—arguably sinful—means, and Jesus was clear about what such greed does to us. It is the barrier that keeps us from entering into God's kingdom.

So in a sense, Christian greed over the past sixteen centuries has helped turn us into something that is un-Christ-like in so many ways that it hardly resembles the early Christian faith from which we came.

Whether this is a good or a bad thing depends on whom you ask. Obviously religious leaders generally decry this as a precipitous moral decline into rampant secularism, but this presumes that the motivations of those at the helm of theocracy had purely noble intentions to begin with. Anytime a system historically leaves millions dead in its wake, it's hard to justify it as entirely altruistic.

This doesn't mean the end of religion in the West, but it does point to the imminence of the end of theocracy, and of the hegemonic reign of Christendom. And with that loosening of our grip on power and material wealth comes a liberating opportunity to embrace, once again, the core message of the Gospel, which calls us to shun such superficial things, because we are supposed to set our gaze on a higher, humbler call.

So what will religious institutions do without the political and social sway they once enjoyed? How will they sustain their institutions that were built to maintain such a dominant presence in the culture? Will the buildings crumble? Some will, yes. But this is a necessary part of the human experience; some might even say it's Biblical.

Consider Jesus' prophecy about the fall of the great temple in Jerusalem. Effectively he was predicting the decline of the theocracy, the dominance of the Jewish church-state, propped up by the Roman Empire. Jesus' Gospel message was, among other things, a message of liberation from such powers, and not only from the political, military, and religious powers themselves, but from the fundamental powers of greed and lust for power that fueled their rise in the first place.

Jesus said that, in the end, not one stone of that magnificent, golden temple on the top of the hill would be left standing because it had become the true god of those in power. And so it was time for a great cleansing, clearing the way for something radically new.

It seems that we've come upon such a time in our history once again. Every religious wall may not fall, every stone may not crumble to dust, but the systems that we have come to worship ahead of God most certainly will come tumbling down.

We can hope that the end of Christendom also heralds the end of institutional Christian greed. But it only presents the opportunity to reset our priorities and to begin to make right some of the harm we've done in serving our misplaced zeal. If the world ever is to see Jesus in our midst again, it will likely not be from behind a gilded pulpit or from within fortified stone walls. Rather, it will be in the empty hands and open arms of those who seek nothing more than to give away love, as if it were the infinitely renewable resource that it actually is.

CHAPTER TEN

HUNGRY AS DOGS

THE CHRIST-LIKE VIRTUE OF CHARITY

Charity, when it immediately comes to mind, conjures images of starving children, abused animals, and possibly tax deductions. For the most part, people react by either reaching for their wallet or putting their hands over it protectively.

In a church setting, it is not about simply putting money in the Sunday offering plate. Yes, as followers of the way of Jesus, we are expected to give generously of our money, but this is a bare-minimum investment; much more is required of us. The opportunities for charity, and the many different definitions of it, are vast. For the intent of this virtue, let's concentrate on going beyond giving to charity, and moving into a more Christ-like life of charity.

THE GOSPEL ACCORDING TO LOUIE

In an episode of his TV show, *Louie,* actor and comedian Louis C.K. is making dinner for his two daughters. He has an extra slice of mango left over after making smoothies for them, and so he offers it to his older daughter. Not surprisingly, the younger one takes some issue with this apparent injustice.

"She got a mango popsicle and I didn't," she whines, "it's not fair!" The so-called popsicle is really just a slice of fruit speared with a fork. But the fact that her sister got one and she didn't makes it the most important slice of mango in the world at this particular moment.

"Look," he says, turning toward her and leaning down to meet her eyes, "the only time you need to worry about your neighbor's bowl is if you're checking to make sure they have enough." Then he turns back to the stove and the girl, a little stunned, walks away.

Any Christian—and arguably, any socially aware human being—would agree that having concern for our neighbor should be a core value of any society. And yet, we hardly have to look beyond the boundaries of our own doorsteps to see evidence all around us that there is unmet need, unnecessary suffering, and unchecked oppression and violence. We know what is right, but we don't really do all we can to make it right.

We might ask ourselves why, save for the fact that the answer we might discover is likely to be one we don't really want to hear: *Drop everything and follow me. Sell all you own and give it to the poor.*

There hardly seems to be a point, though. I could sell all of my worldly possessions, give them to people in need, and there would still be an overwhelming amount of need, right there in front of me. Not only that, but now I'm among the poor, vulnerable, and in need of help. Plus I've lost the means to keep giving, because now I've given up all I had. Maybe it makes more sense to stay where I am, carve a little bit off the top (well, maybe not off the very top, but after I make sure the basics are covered for me and my loved ones), give it to a good cause, and then go about my business of making more with the intent of giving some more. Once I get more, that is.

Author Jack London says, "A bone to the dog is not charity. Charity is the bone shared with the dog, when you are just as hungry as the dog." We may be willing to give from what's left, but this isn't the sort of sacrificial generosity to which we're called by Jesus' example. Our world tells us that the one who dies with the most toys wins, but the message of Jesus is different; if one is suffering, we all fall short.

Giving something to charity isn't really the same as living every day with a charitable heart. Granted, we are called to give generously to others from what we have, but a charitable heart goes further. But we are also called to change the systems we live in which cause the inequities in the first place. The challenge is deeper, more complex, and more personal than this. We can give large sums of money to a good cause or dedicate our lives to social justice work, and yet the notion of Christ-like charity can elude us.

WE, THE SYSTEM

Speaker, pastor, and activist David Moore argues that Christianity has become so inured to the values and effects of capitalism within our religious institutions that we're effectively blind to its presence:

> What concerns me as a pastor is we have merged religion with hyper-capitalism to develop a sacrosanct and unassailable construct, and if anyone questions it,

they are dismissed as un-American, a class warrior, or a Marxist. And Christians buy and sell that construct.[1]

Moore suggests that we enter into an implied social contract with the power-bearing institutions and systems in our lives. How this functions: we do not threaten their existence, and in exchange, they help us feel satisfied and good about ourselves. This may sound particularly cynical on the surface, but consider, for a moment, the following parallels:

A clothing company has a shirt to sell. To close the deal, they must offer you the greatest perceived value at the lowest possible cost. The actual price is on the sticker. In the free market system where competition is fierce, these companies strain for every advantage possible by keeping labor, material, and distribution costs low. Savvier consumers express concerns about where the raw materials are sourced, whether the labor conditions of workers are fair, and if the company's business model is environmentally friendly. Most of us, however, know little or nothing about the products we buy on a daily basis. If the seller makes us feel good about our purchase, all the better. In the last decade, we have been trained to check for key terms such as "fair trade," "organic," or "eco-friendly," but we're only willing to pay so much for these add-ons. Ultimately, the transaction is consummated as long as the company can make us feel good enough about the purchase to hand over our money and think little about how it was sourced.

Another example: A political party has a candidate they are positioning for public office. In order to gain the office, they have to secure a certain number of votes. To do that, they have to campaign, which costs money. To inspire people to action, they cast a grand vision, telling you that you're an integral part of that vision. We are the agents of change and transformation for which you long, they claim. All they need from you in order to make that happen is your vote, perhaps a contribution, and maybe a few hours on the ground in your neighborhood on behalf of your candidate. In exchange, the political system will validate your efforts and reward your faithfulness by assuring you that you are the inspiration at the heart of the movement. By taking a little bit of time and money to support the campaign, you are ensuring that all the values you hold dear will finally be realized.

Your church does good things in the community. They have a food pantry, an annual mission trip to South America, and 10 percent of all offerings that come in go back out to local and global mission projects. In fact, they've recently embarked on a capital campaign to add a new wing to the facility, which will house a gym that will be open to the community three evenings a week. What is required of you is that you lend your support in the form of an additional tithe, ongoing prayer, and maybe a few hours on the weekends to help with painting and landscaping. You maintain your present way of life while also helping out an institution whose mission you believe is worthwhile. And on Sundays, the pastor assures you that you are, indeed, living out the call of Christ to serve those in need.

In each of these scenarios, though it may be subtle, the pattern is clear. In each case, we're engaging in a transaction. Each time, the system requires something from us, and in order to achieve a desired goal, it offers you the highest perceived reward at the lowest possible cost. The transaction takes place when you lend your support and/or resources to the system (be it political, economic, or religious), and the system, in turn, validates your commitment and helps you feel good about your decision.

The problem arises when it becomes clear that a system's primary goal is not the ideals set forth to the consumer (your purchase helps save rain forests; your vote ensures justice for the oppressed; your tithe feeds the "least of these"), but rather the perpetuation of the system itself.

It's easy to vilify "the system," as if it were some abstract entity with a will of its own. But at the heart of every institutional organization are human hearts, minds, and ambitions. We are, in effect, "the system."

OUR FOUR REPONSES

There are four responses to perceived injustice, suffering, violence, or inequality to consider. In some instances, Christianity addresses these well; other times, not so much. Often, we respond with some combination of the following, and yet we fail to effect the kind of real, radical change we're called to as followers of Christ:

1. Freely giving time and material wealth toward a worthwhile cause
2. Earnestly working for systemic change (i.e., social justice) to rectify the imbalance in the existing systems
3. Honestly identifying and confessing the complicity we have in being a part of corrupt systems that lead to the kind of violence, inequity, oppression, and injustice we claim to want to fix
4. Actively seeking to subvert the system entirely, acknowl-

edging that it is inherently built on a set of values and principles that perpetuate the injustice

In general, most churches or denominations work well with the first kind of response. It would be hard to find a church without some kind of community outreach, either in the form of monetary gifts, community service work, or a combination of the two. But statistically at least, the issue of how deeply committed we are to charity is debatable. The United Nations estimates that the entirety of the world's hunger problems could be solved with an annual budget of approximately $30 billion.[2] Meanwhile, a recent study by *The Economist* magazine estimated that the Catholic Church in the United States alone had an annual combined budget of $170 billion in 2010, when all of the assets of the Church are considered together.[3] So in theory, by allocating about *one-sixth* of the total budget of the Catholic Church in the United States to solving hunger (not counting any other denominations, religions, or even Catholic institutions outside the United States), hunger could conceivably disappear from the face of the earth.

And it turns out we think we're much more generous than we actually are. According to blogger David Briggs, a recent "Science of Generosity Survey" conducted by Notre Dame University found that, although one-fourth of Christian churchgoers claimed to tithe (give at least 10 percent of their income to their church), only three out of a hundred of us actually give at least half that much, according to our tax returns.[4]

Some churches try to go a step further, seeking to effect change in the existing systems so that greater balance and equity may be realized. Consider the "four responses" to injustice I just mentioned. A movement took hold in the early twentieth century primarily in Protestant churches in the United States called the Social Gospel. The idea was fairly simple: apply Christian ethics and values to the social woes facing the culture around us. The movement challenged the existing notion that Christianity's primary goal was to save souls and convert people. It focused instead on invoking a more perfect vision of "God's kingdom come" by helping set right the injustices in our social and economic systems. This was done through nonviolent means such as marches, protests, legal advocacy, and boycotts, among other things.

The effort, spearheaded by leaders such as Walter Rauschenbusch and Martin Luther King Jr., made remarkable strides in civil rights and eradicating the practice of child labor. Rauschenbusch's work in the Hell's Kitchen neighborhood on behalf of the poor in New York inspired others to replicate such models of embedded urban assistance and advocacy nationwide. King's vision and leadership helped coordinate efforts to successfully integrate everything from public schools to public spaces of all types. But though effective in refocusing the Church in some ways on its Gospel mission beyond the walls, the Social Gospel made grossly idealistic assumptions about the systems they sought to change. Granted, it addressed gaping wounds evident within the political and economic systems in America, but it fell short of pulling back the curtain entirely, exposing the reality that *the problems were inherent in the very political, religious, and economic systems themselves.*

Serving a meal to someone who is hungry doesn't take

on the systemic imbalances of privilege and opportunity that hold that person in the grip of poverty, perhaps for a lifetime, or even multiple generations to follow. And racial integration, though creating an opportunity for equity, doesn't automatically change the hearts of those who deem people from other races to be somehow inferior.

It is not realistic to assume that the systemic corruption surrounding us can be corrected until we first correct our own corruption. When it comes to sin, modern Western Christianity has missed the mark on two big counts. First, there's the issue of priorities. We've focused far more on sexual morality than on any other kind of sin. For example, the Church traditionally finds it easier to talk about the supposed evils of homosexuality or premarital sex rather than the sin of environmental abuse or generational cycles of poverty. It's much easier, after all, to condemn individual behavior rather than galvanize a populace to radical change.

Second, we have remained woefully obsessed with individual sin, largely ignoring the collective responsibility we have for the world's suffering. I am much more likely to be judged by my church family for buying pornography than I am for putting gas in my car, never mind if more people were displaced, tortured, or even killed in order for me to fill my tank.

BE AN ANT

One of my favorite children's church stories involves an ant farm. The teacher shows the ants scurrying around inside the self-forged ant maze and asks the children if they think that God loves the ants. Generally, the kids say yes, except for the ones who prefer to singe the little buggers with a magnifying glass, but they're going to Hell anyway.

"Let's tell the ants that God loves them," the teacher says, holding the farm down at their level, at which point the kids burst forth in a chorus of divine ant admiration.

"The problem is," says the teacher, "the ants don't speak our language. They don't understand. What would we have to do in order to be able to really tell them God loves them?"

"Become an ant?" some precocious squirt inevitably says at this point.

One of my favorite passages in Scripture comes from the very first few verses of the Gospel of John:

> *In the beginning was the Word, and the Word was with God, and the Word was God. He was in the beginning with God. All things came into being through him, and without him not one thing came into being....And the Word became flesh and lived among us...*

Imagine a God whose love is so great that it broke through into the world with skin on. Speaking our words, walking our steps, sharing our meals, telling our stories. It's one thing to be given all that creation affords us as an extravagant gift; it's another altogether to be told and shown, face to face, by the One who gave you that gift, that you are loved beyond your wildest imagination.

A truly charitable heart finds its foundation in real compassion, and real compassion is found through humble confession. The only way to have that kind of compassion is to identify as fully as possible with both the humanity and the divinity of the people you claim to care about.

Hopefully I employ that privilege to make the kind of changes in the world that level the rules of the game a little more. Hopefully I'll consume less, give more, and actually mean it when I say that, while even one still suffers, I continue to fall short.

It's interesting that the verse offered by Paul in 1 Corinthians 13:13 is pretty different when you compare translations. First, from the King James version:

> And now abideth faith, hope, charity, these three; but the greatest of these is charity.

But when we get a more modern translation, such as the New Revised Standard Version, charity is replaced:

> And now faith, hope, and love abide, these three; and the greatest of these is love.

This is an example of where our Western, contemporary understanding of "love" falls short. We tend to think of it more as a feeling, or as romantic love. But the Greek language has three words for love: *eros* (romantic love), *philios* (brotherly love), and *agape* (the kind of love revealed by Jesus). In this verse, the kind of love being referred to is *agape*, which can be translated either as "love" or "charity."

This is because *agape* is not something we feel; it is something we do. Agape is a covenant we make with the world, to live by the example of selfless sacrifice modeled for us by Jesus. It can't be fully realized with a check in the offering plate; agape requires all of us. So to live out the call to Christian charity—which Paul argues is the most important virtue of the faith—we have to invest ourselves fully in this promise to throw our whole selves into a way of life that is radically generous with all that we are and all that we have.

When asked what was required of us in order to embody this kind of love—this *agape*—Jesus was clear: it takes everything.

CHAPTER ELEVEN

IF ONLY THEY WERE (FILL IN THE BLANK)

THE CHRISTIAN SCANDAL OF JUDGMENT

We all do it. Everyone judges somebody else. Even if it's simply that we hold contempt for those who judge others, we're still a part of the problem. But why? What is it in our nature that feels such a profound need to place a value on the lives and behaviors of others? Part of it is rooted in basic evolution. We're constantly critiquing our environment and the groups with which we identify ourselves. We want to find some assurance that we're making good decisions, ones that will contribute to our happiness, well-being, and longevity. From political parties to athletic jerseys, musical preferences, and even houses of worship, we need to feel as if the brands we like, or people with whom we are associated, are the best.

In order to be the best, of course, everything else has to be somehow inferior. We seek out justifications for the superiority of our own choices, while rooting around for flaws in the affiliations of others. On the most basic level, it is simply not possible *not* to do it; it's fundamental to human nature. Because if we're not aligned with what we perceive to be the best, most proper, correct, or perhaps even the *only* way of doing things, it reflects poorly on our own sense of judgment.

Let's consider the Church in particular. We have parsed ourselves into so many subdivisions based on our differences that it's hard to keep track of exactly how many different denominations there are within the Christian faith alone. There are hundreds of subgroups just among Baptists, and some theological scholars peg the total number of Christian denominations at upwards of 34,000 worldwide.[1]

Every single one of these groups thinks they are somehow different, and arguably superior, to the other 33,999. There would be no point in separating and establishing their group if this was not the case. In fact, there is a great deal of debate within the wider Christian community about which denominations are technically even Christian. Some denominations readily condemn other denominations and leaders for leading people straight to Hell.

As if we didn't have enough internal divisions, there's the matter of those who are not yet saved: the great unwashed. The millions among us who risk an eternity of fiery suffering unless we bring them into the fold. They are the ones whom we must make more like us. We are commanded by the Gospel to assimilate them so that they will join us in paradise. Until that time when they are converted, we judge them for their faithlessness.

If only *they* could see the error of their ways. If only *they* understood the true consequences of their decisions. If only *they* had a glimpse of Hell, they'd come running to church, begging for the salvation required to remain in God's favor.

I once heard a Sunday school teacher tell a six-year-old in her class that talking to his friend might cause that friend to stumble, to miss out on the one and only chance for eternal salvation. And was the bit of gossip or the fart joke he felt compelled to share at such a crucial time really worth the possible destruction of his immortal soul?

Of course, if we approach Scripture as if it were a single, static document, we can find plenty of justification for the depiction of God as an angry, judgmental being. Consider the creation story involving Adam and Eve, the basis for the concept of original sin, or the idea that we all bear an indelible mark of brokenness thanks to God's curse on the first two people and every single one of their ancestors for all of time. Then there's the condemnation of Nineveh, the destruction of Sodom and Gomorrah, the great flood story...the list goes on and on. If we care to see God as judgmental and punishing, we have our support all over the place in the Bible.

But one of the most valuable things about the Bible is that it also reveals the different ways people thought of themselves and God at different points throughout history. And given the great shifts from the early Hebrew texts to the Gospels and Pauline letters, clearly those perceptions changed over time. In a sense, the Bible is a story of our spiritual, social, and theological evolution. But oftentimes, we mistakenly engage the Bible as if it is not a progressive text, in the sense that it begins in one place, but takes us somewhere quite different.

Historically, the Church has resisted a progressive approach to Scripture, such as when Christian leaders judged Copernicus as a heretic for suggesting the earth wasn't at the center of the universe. It was only once the evidence was overwhelming that religious leaders finally conceded that he might actually be right. And we have plenty of other examples, even today, of the friction between contemporary thought and a more arcane interpretation of the sacred texts.

For example, Christianity has been infamously judgmental of sexuality, particularly outside the context of marriage. However, much of this judgment comes from the refusal to abandon some clearly outmoded understandings of simple biology or archaeology. For example, a good number of Christians consider masturbation to be a sin. Perhaps fewer, but still many millions, agree that the use of contraception is contrary to God's law. Since 1968, the Catholic Church has explicitly stated that the use of contraception is considered a sin and is counter to Biblical and Church teaching.[2] Protestant Christian leaders vary widely on this matter, though some of the more conservative Christian authorities still embrace this Catholic mandate.

However, much of this judgment comes from an often-misunderstood text, popularly described as the "sin of Onan."

In the Bible, a man named Onan marries the sister of his now-deceased former wife, according to the custom of the day. Onan's sin is that he intentionally ejaculates in such a way that he prevents his new wife from getting pregnant, because he knew the child would not be his (the culture would have recognized it as his brother's baby). For this transgression, he is killed by God.[*] For some, this is clear evidence that any sexual act outside the effort to create new life is morally reprehensible. But we have to keep in mind that, given the patriarchal systems of the day, it was believed that the man contained the entire human embryo within his semen. Therefore, if he ever ejaculated without creating life, he

---

[*] Genesis 38:8-10

was effectively committing murder. Now, given our advances in science, we know better than this today, and yet the judgments on such matters of sexual morality persist.

For a further example, it's hard to believe that in the twenty-first century we're still debating whether the earth is billions of years old, or if it was literally created in seven days some five millennia ago. The Biblical creation stories predate so much modern progress in the disciplines of archaeology, astronomy, anthropology, biology, and physics. But rather than framing the narratives of the Bible within the progressive framework of human understanding, proponents of literal Biblical creationism deem the preponderance of scientific knowledge to be a diabolical effort to debunk the very existence of God.

We tend to judge that which we fear. It is a basic tendency within all human beings. But when the desire to cling to an antiquated understanding of sacred texts supersedes our ability to reconcile common sense with our philosophical and religious narratives, an unnecessary schism occurs, with harsh judgments flying from both sides about who is right.

To understand why people see God as a judgmental being, it is helpful to consider how God is portrayed in much of the Old Testament. In the story of Adam and Eve, God is portrayed as a person walking around the Garden of Eden, much like his new creations. Personally, I can't help picturing this God in a long, white bathrobe with some thong sandals, and I'm guessing many of you have a similar image. From here, God becomes slightly more removed, depicted as speaking through a burning bush, from within clouds or bright lights on a mountaintop, or through people's dreams. Despite the growing abstraction, this God is still heavily, directly involved in the daily operations of the world.

But then, inevitably, bad stuff happens. Famines and droughts parch the land, invading armies topple cities, and an entire nation of people are forced into slavery, and then cast into decades of exile. Given such a hands-on understanding of God, this must mean either that God made these things happen, or at the very least, God allowed them to happen. The fifty-cent word for this conundrum in theological circles is "theodicy": how we reconcile the idea of a loving God with the fact that there is tragedy and suffering in the world.

The answer, in most cases in the Old Testament in particular, is that it's our fault. We've done something to displease God, and therefore our punishment is the bad thing portrayed in the story. We are left with a God that loves us, but that cannot tolerate our sinfulness. Therefore, some price must be paid for the wrongdoing. In many cases, this was the explanation for things like the invasion of Judah by the Babylonians and the forty years of desert wandering by the Jews following their release from Egyptian captivity. God's judgment on humanity must be satisfied.

In the Christian context, the result of clinging to a theology of judgment when we think about God and interpret Scripture is that we create for ourselves an angry God who keeps an account of our wrongdoing and requires some payment for these transgressions. We see in the crucifixion a necessary sacrifice, required by God of his own son, in order to atone for the sins of humanity. And based on particular interpretations of select Scriptures, many Christians believe in a literal, physical place of fiery torment where those unwilling to seek forgiveness for their sinfulness will pay the ultimate price, thus justifying our own faithfulness and ensuring that each person gets what we believe they deserve.

First, we have to consider what we mean when we are talking about the judgment of God. There are many expressions of judgment throughout Scripture, but rather than thinking of judgment in monolithic terms, consider that there are examples of both retributive judgment and restorative judgment in the Bible.

Retributive judgment claims that an eye for an eye is the rule of law.[3] Restorative judgment deems that a man's love for his son is greater than his anger at his son's propensity for blowing his inheritance and coming back empty-handed.[4] Judgment based on retribution scatters the tribes who built the Tower of Babel out of pride, fracturing them into a splintered cultural diaspora for trying to be like God.[5] A judge intent on restoration, however, uses those same languages to inspire the disciples at Pentecost to spread the unifying, merciful message of the Gospel to all the nations.[6]

There are various degrees and schools of thought on both ideas, but to put it in the simplest of terms, retributive judgment is principally concerned with making things *fair*. Restorative judgment, on the other hand, is focused on making things *right* or *whole*.

With retributive judgment, there is a price to be paid for every wrong, and that balance must be pursued until those who were wronged are satisfied. Let the punishment fit the crime, says retributive judgment. The story of Noah and the flood is the most popular example of this.[7] Humanity is screwing up on a global scale, so God decides to wipe the slate clean. And given an understanding of a hands-on God, we have to work through why something like a horrible flood would come along and kill so many people. But consider that the authors of such stories are not on the scene, reporting this as it happens in real time. They are looking back at tragedy on a massive scale and asking "why?"

Restorative judgment is not quite as straightforward. It goes deeper and broader, seeking to better understand the context in which the offense took place to begin with, and then to address the fundamental root causes that led to the problem.

Consider this simple example: A poor person who lives on the streets of a city steals a loaf of bread from a local market. Though both kinds of judgment recognize that this presents a problem, they address that problem very differently. Retributive judgment says that the man who stole the bread has broken the law, taking something that isn't his. He must make this right by dealing with a punishment that is deemed consistent with the wrong he did to the storeowner. He may be required to pay a fine, or even spend time in jail. But in the end, the man who stole the bread is still hungry and without the prospect for a meal by other means, and the shopkeeper still doesn't have his stolen loaf of bread back. The problems that led to the crime still exist, though the parties involved can claim that justice has been done.

Restorative judgment explores beneath the surface, asking questions like *What led the man to his state of desperation in the first place? Was he suffering from untreated issues with mental health or addiction? Had he been the victim of the economic downturn?* While not excusing the wrongdoing, restorative judgment recognizes, in a broader context, that there are far larger, more complex and pressing issues that beg our attention, well beyond the particular transgression in question.

Restorative judgment doesn't seek to repay wrong with

appropriate punishment; it seeks to undermine the entire system of retributive judgment to incline the course of humanity toward an ultimate resolution. Retributive judgment is punitive in nature; it requires satisfaction. Restorative judgment, however, is discerning, surgical, and strategic in helping free people from self-perpetuating systems of brokenness and our seemingly hopeless enslavement to our own desire.

We should also consider the emphasis of Jesus' ministry. Was Jesus more concerned with retribution or with restoration? Consider Jesus' command to turn the other cheek when we are offended, rather than striking back in kind. Or consider that, at his moment of greatest suffering, while coming to terms with the inevitability of his own death, he uses his final breaths to beg forgiveness for those who unjustly murdered and abandoned him.

If Jesus expects us to move beyond a social dynamic of retributive judgment (an eye for an eye) and toward a gospel of restoration ("Father, forgive them, for they know not what they do"), why should we expect any less from the God we claim created us in a like image?

The Christian vision for God's kingdom should be one of "jubilee," which was a concept within ancient Jewish culture that, every fifty years, one year should be spent in intentional rest. Slaves also were to be freed, debts forgiven, and land returned to prior owners. Rather than satisfying our desire for retributive justice, this kingdom vision is one in which all people are freed from the hunger, the fundamental enslavement to desire that perpetuates individual and systemic behaviors mired in sin and brokenness. When considered within the context of this hunger, retributive judgment is merely an extension of our ongoing desire to slake and, once and for all, silence the hunger. It is our hope that this kind of a judgment will finally make us feel whole, but it never does.

We see patterns of progression throughout Scripture away from retributive judgment and toward one of restoration, finally perfected in the life and teachings of Jesus. As Jesus himself says, this is not abolition of the old ways, but rather a process of more fully realizing their purpose. We progress from a rule of law toward a rule of love.

The only thing that breaks the cycle of sin is a love that transcends our earthly desire. It is the all-consuming, perfect love described in 1 John 4:18, which reminds us that there is no fear in love. We can be governed either by fear or love, but we can't cling to both. A restorative sense of judgment is one of discernment and wisdom, steeped in mercy and perfect love. Restorative judgment does not require fairness to be meted out in human terms; it casts a broader vision, in which the sum total of our self-imposed brokenness can, indeed, be made whole.

Such is the judgment of a God of restoration, of "Thy kingdom come, thy will be done, on earth as it is in heaven." We are restored to wholeness, both individually and collectively, when we fully embrace God's judgment in this sense. But in order to do so, we must first abandon our limited, human notions of what judgment looks like.

When we do, we become a little bit more like the Christ we claim. We live out such restorative judgment in our daily lives, mending divisions, offering radically unconditional love and mercy to our enemy. We begin to see the world as God sees it: with no lines.

CHAPTER TWELVE

NINJA JESUS

THE CHRIST-LIKE VIRTUE OF MERCY

If we have power, our cultural norms suggest we should use it. If we have a leg up on someone else, take advantage. But there is a curious strength in withholding power in mercy. There are examples of this throughout the Bible.

In Genesis, God tells Adam and Eve to keep away from the Tree of Knowledge, or else they will die. They do it anyway, and despite their screwups, God offers them mercy. Their actions certainly weren't without any consequence, but immediate, physical death wasn't among them. The story of Noah and the flood is a fairly chilling account of mass extinction, but on the other hand, God deems that there still is something worth saving in humanity. God allows for a fresh start with Noah and his family, and also vows that such a catastrophe will never befall humanity again.

Reading the story of God ordering Abraham to sacrifice his son, Isaac, without any broader context seems to portray the God of Israel as—to put it bluntly—kind of a jerk. But when we realize that child sacrifice was a common practice among many of the baalite (read: non-Jewish) religions at the time, and consider that God ultimately stopped Abraham from killing Isaac, we can see that at the heart of the story is God's desire for faithfulness, not blood sacrifice. This would be an act of infinite mercy for those who felt they needed to offer up their own children to an otherwise bloodthirsty God.

This is the portrayal of a God that cultivates faithfulness through such acts of mercy, rather than through coercion by fear. But Biblical mercy is more than an act of kindness, or even a strategic means of reconciling God's people to God. It can be, when applied in the right way, a creatively subversive means of throwing unjust systems that divide, oppress, and show no mercy themselves into disarray. Mercy calls us not just to step outside the circle, and not simply to bring others back into it, but to destroy the boundary altogether, forever.

A THIRD WAY

The Bible seems not just to tolerate violence; in some instances, it appears to celebrate it. Even David, the famed king of the Jewish people, makes his debut in the texts by killing a giant warrior. So maybe violence does have some redemptive qualities after all!

Some see it differently.

In holding Peter back from killing the Roman soldiers who came to take him away for crucifixion, Jesus not only spared the life of an enemy, but exposed the role of the Roman occupiers as unjust oppressors. Had he or his disciples struck out in violence, the Romans would have been justified in their persecution of Jesus. But by offering his captors mercy, he lived out the mandate of the Gospel to love our enemies, while also pointing to the inherent self-serving—some might say sinful—dynamics at the heart of the empire.

When we engage in mercy, however, we become vulnerable. We can't control the offenses toward us if we do not retaliate. It's a tough sell. Jesus entered Jerusalem for the last time to a parade of palm branches and shouts of "hosanna," which means "save us." But the call was not for a spiritual or existential salvation; the people of occupied Israel hoped for Jesus to enter as a conquering hero. When he refused, they turned their backs on him. They sought a leader emboldened by a vision to conquer their oppressor, and he rejected this as a perpetuation of the problem that led to such subjugation in the first place. The proverbial tables had to be overturned; it wasn't sufficient to simply trade out the table settings. And today, when we resort to military might (or even the threat of force) to impose our will or maintain the status quo, we turn our backs on the same Christ who calls us to change the rules, and not just the rulers. Consider that we spend twenty times more in the United States' annual budget on military force than we do on international aid. If where we place our money speaks to our priorities as a nation, preservation of our present way of life far outweighs a Christ-like justice for others.

But there is strength in the type of mercifully subversive resistance modeled by Jesus. Returning to Walter Wink, he points out in his book *Jesus and Nonviolence: A Third Way*, the ultimate goal isn't to win, but rather to reconcile:

> Jesus did not advocate nonviolence merely as a technique for outwitting the enemy, but as a just means of opposing the enemy in such a way as to hold open the

possibility of the enemy's becoming just as well. Both sides must win.[1]

Talk about radical! To engage your oppressor not just with the goal of nonviolent disarmament, but also with the aim of making the division between you disappear, is revolutionary.

COWARDICE VS. MERCY

When I was in middle school, I joined the wrestling team. I was not good, but I had to participate in something. Fortunately wrestling made room for kids of all sizes, even scrawny and gangly. So I was in.

Andrew, my sparring partner, made a regular habit of pinning me in a matter of seconds. But one time, while we were in a match in front of the whole class, I found myself on top of Andrew by way of some minor miracle. Andrew, being fiery-tempered, exploded as soon as I let him up. He punched me, to which I responded by walking away and bleeding in silence. When I told my dad about what happened over dinner that night, he was stunned. He ordered me to go back to school the next day and fight Andrew, but I never did.

The parallel between my situation with Andrew and a Christ-like model of nonviolent engagement might seem obvious, but there's a huge difference. For one, I walked away because I was afraid. That's cowardice, not mercy. Jesus' model of strength is to stand strong in the face of violence, to redirect the energy aimed to harm you, and to hold out hope, even in the most hopeless situation, that healing is possible.

Even if you don't buy into this theory of radical nonviolence, the result of Jesus' nonviolent engagement was still the same: the Roman Empire—the most powerful in the world at the time—was threatened enough by his life and teaching that they were compelled to kill him. At the same time, a movement was born that no act of force or violence can dispel. Other religions have similar champions. They saw beyond personal consequences, realizing that there can be something greater at stake than our own safety or comfort.

Responding to violence with something other than violence shows greater strength than flexing physical muscle. The issue, however, is that our culture doesn't agree with this approach. There's a word for guys who get beat up and don't fight back, and it's not meant to be flattering. I don't know what the Hebrew equivalent to this was, but I'm guessing Jesus got called something along these lines on more than one occasion. One of the many great things about him was that he didn't care what culture told him he had to be. He found his strength and his identity from within himself, endowed, as he believed, by God.

Jesus' nonviolent stance seems to contradict other Scriptural texts. Should we just chalk this up as yet another one of the many times when the Bible contradicted itself? It's actually an example of the Bible being progressive, taking us from one place to another. In this case, that progress is from a value system of violence-based judgment and retribution toward a Gospel-inspired vision of empire-shaking peace. This kind of shift in human values makes room for God to inspire hope in the midst of suffering, and to spark our collective creative imaginations so we can break our old, violent, retributive cycles.

PERFECTION IN PROGRESS

It is worth remembering that many different people wrote the Bible over generations, in different cultures and even different languages. Envisioning Scripture as a long, gradually evolving timeline helps us understand Jesus' apparent opposition to the Old Testament texts. In the original Old Testament laws, there is a sevenfold vengeance that is practiced. If someone kills one of your goats, you have the right to kill seven of his. If someone insults your wife, you burn down his house.

Rather than stemming an escalation of violence, such laws served only to inflame the problem. At some point in history, the "eye for an eye" rule was inserted. Given the backdrop of sevenfold vengeance to consider this, we might better understand this famous law as something more like "no more than an eye for an eye."

Thus began a more civilized—even "just"—approach to retribution, particularly in a culture that did not have an established judicial system.

Understanding this, Jesus' command to turn the other cheek makes sense as the next logical step toward a greater peace. When someone would slap another person in Jesus' culture, they used their right hand to do so. The left hand was employed for many undignified—or even unhygienic—acts, but striking someone wasn't one of them. By turning the other cheek, it forced an offender to use the back of their right hand if they wanted to strike again. It was illegal to strike an equal (or anyone other than a slave) with the back of your hand, so if the person you're striking turned their cheek, you either had to break the law or abstain (which was considered cowardice). So they were effectively stuck, disarmed, without their victim raising a hand to them in response.

This form of nonviolent resistance is strength expressed through the restraint of power. Mercy is modeled by holding out the hope that equality—something our world says is impossible—can be realized.

THEOPOETICS AS A THIRD WAY

Christianity generally has been strong—at least in principle—on the notion of mercy for the weak or oppressed. Such commandments are undeniably explicit in the teachings of Christ. But mercy centered on the hope of restoration can't stop merely at acts of charity. We can't convince ourselves that simply by feeding the poor, or visiting the lonely and imprisoned, we are fulfilling Jesus' commandment to love our neighbor. If our mercy stops at charity, we fail to address the root causes that imprisoned those people or sent them into poverty. We have to imagine a better world, in which such systemic violence and oppression cannot stand, and then we have to work tirelessly to realize that vision.

But the mercy of restorative justice is about more than tearing down the powers that be so that the oppressed may rise up over their oppressors. That, after all, is only a perpetuation of the sort of retributive justice we're called away from. Truly restorative justice claims that oppressor and victim can, and ultimately must, coexist as equals, with no winners and losers. But such an approach is doubly merciful, in that it not only liberates the victim from further violence and oppression, but also spares the perpetrator the dire consequences of their own actions, based on the very system within which they were operating.

Walter Wink, as well as other creative nonviolent activists, suggests that when we think we have only two options in responding to violence or oppression in our world—respond in kind to violence, or do nothing—it is because of a lack of creative imagination. We see examples of such creative imagination throughout Jesus' ministry. There were attempts to trap him within a dichotomous legal argument. The Pharisees asked theological questions with the aim of committing blasphemy. But time and again, Jesus left his opponents dumbfounded, finding instead a "third way" to address their challenges. A way they had not considered.

Jesus often surprised his friends and enemies alike by offering healing and mercy not just to those whom they would expect; rather, he went out of his way to reach out and offer the same graces to the non-Jews, the outcasts, the diseased and stigmatized. In doing so, he was offering more than help to one person; he was interrupting the entire social order by demonstrating that God's mercy extends beyond all human-made boundaries. As my wife, Amy, has said more than once, we're not called as Christians simply to make a difference in the world; we're called to make a different world entirely.

This kind of mandate requires at its heart a sort of creative imagination, one that can envisage both victim and perpetrator at peace with each other. It also requires us to let go of previous notions of an anthropomorphic God, with equally human notions of right, wrong, fairness, and justice. Within postmodern theological circles, there is a movement called theopoetics. It is a means to escape the tendency of confining

God's essence and the call of Christ to a modernist, binary, rationally bound (and painfully human) context.

When Jesus was questioned about the kingdom of God, he drew comparative illustrations, saying it was like a pearl, or a seed or a tree. Was it literally a seed? Probably not, but his rhetorical technique was effective at painting a picture. And the mental images he evoked pointed to dimensions or attributes of things that people were voraciously curious about, but which they could not possibly imagine in their entirety. So the question at the heart of theopoetics is how to engage people with concepts that they cannot possibly understand with their rational minds.

The practice of theopoetics employs art in all its forms as a means to stir the human soul, and to orient the spirit and ignite the imagination for something previously unimagined, such as a social order in which conqueror and victim mercifully coexist.

To that end, theopoetics has to be *apocryphal*, meaning that it has to touch on that which is hidden. It must also be *apocalyptic*, in that it helps to unveil something to us or in us, to awaken the heart to a call for justice, healing, and reconciliation, to see the potential for mercy, even when our instincts are to seek a more human understanding of justice. And finally, theopoetics should be *prophetic*. It needs to call us to account when we lapse into cycles of violence and endless retribution. It should reveal in our midst our own potential to act as the oppressor over our brothers and sisters. It helps pull back the curtain of self-deception and justification, calling us, over and again, back to the mercy that rests at the heart of Jesus' Gospel message.

If the Christian faith cannot keep such a vision at its heart, we have no true role in the forthcoming kingdom of God. We are nothing more than an extension of the empire we're called to challenge. Rather than being the manifestation of Christ's mercy to a world so desperately in need, we help perpetuate the broken and unjust systems that have proved throughout history never to satisfy our desperate longing for something greater. We become a barrier to the coming of God's merciful kingdom, rather than its stewards.

CHAPTER THIRTEEN

MILLIONS IN THE HANDS OF AN ANGRY GOD

THE CHRISTIAN SCANDAL OF FEAR

Fear is a substrate emotion. Oftentimes, when a strong feeling is experienced—particularly a negative one—it is rooted in fear. Such is the case with many of the vices and scandals of our faith; each has a foundation built on fear of some kind and on some level, be it fear of loss, vulnerability, humiliation, death, or loneliness.

In many respects, Christianity has historically been intent on addressing these fears, focusing on rewards beyond our present life, the immortality of the soul, and the ever-present God who will never abandon us. On the other side of that coin, many church leaders have found fear to be one of the most powerful tools both to recruit and control their faithful. Though a few may use fear with clearly malicious intent, most leaders likely believe they are doing people a favor by "scaring them straight." Their intentions, though misguided, are well meaning. Without such firm redirection, the inevitable consequence is a kind of eternal conscious torment described in Chapter Eleven.

Recent studies have found that what we believe *about* God actually has a strong, measurable effect on our mental health and emotional well-being in this life, which begs the question: Is fear necessary as part of our faith, or does it do more harm than good?

IN THE HANDS OF AN ANGRY GOD

I grew up in an extremely conservative denomination, memorizing Scripture as part of what was referred to as "sword drills," and arming myself with the necessary tools to convert my friends to the side of righteousness. The Bible was a critical means to that end of saving souls, and so it was important to know it well.

We learned to memorize it but not question it. We were taught to absorb it without nuance, without curiosity about deeper meaning, cultural context, or possible human agenda. We learned that the earth was five thousand years old, that scientists fabricated the fossil record to fit their agenda, and that some people—actually, most people—were going to Hell.

My Jewish friends were all going to Hell for sure, as was my father, since he wasn't a churchgoing, God-fearing kind of guy. And if I wasn't careful, I'd be next. As a young boy who didn't understand the mind games at play, there were nights when I would wake up, shaking in my bed from dreams of the hungry flames of Hell licking at my heels. My daily decisions were increasingly governed by fear and guilt rather than by love or a sense of what was right.

The God of my understanding was a terrible, jealous, ferocious creature. He hungered for vengeance, called for the death of his innocent son, and condemned much of his own beloved creation to eternal suffering, supposedly because this creation employed the free will he had afforded them to go it alone and pursue that which was beyond God's protection and grace.

The lines between Heaven and Hell were clear and stark. One's primary mission on any given day was to ensure one's position on the right side of that line. Second to that was to bring as many other people as possible over to that same side before the wrath of God rained down in plumes of fire and smoldering sulfur.

I was sure I didn't want any part of it near me.

ANATOMY OF FEAR

The experience of fear manifests itself in a very primitive part of the brain called the amygdala. Located deep in the center of our brains, as well as the brains of all complex vertebrates, this region is responsible for, among other things, memory and emotion. The activity of this part of the brain can occur beyond the conscious reasoning of the cerebral cortex, where more complex cognitive functions happen.

Our amygdala is where our "fight or flight" reflex comes from. It is the source of that rush of adrenaline, the increased heartbeat, and rapid breathing when someone startles you. In addition to fear, it is the central processing station for things like aggression, desire, anxiety, and even addiction. Such impulses, feelings, and responses are beyond rationality, and are deeply embedded in our nature. They have tremendous power over how we act, and they can have a profound effect on everything from our personality to our mental health.

In other words, the part of the brain where fear manifests

itself is, quite literally, at the core of who and what we are. It can lead us to do incredible things, terrible things, and the effects of fear can change the course of our lives forever.

In 2006, the Baylor Institute for Studies of Religion conducted a national survey of 1,721 randomly sampled respondents about how they understand God, along with scores of questions about everything from their educational background to their political affiliation. The study also looked at religious habits, including how often people prayed, went to church, and read Scripture. They found that the single most significant factor in predicting people's behavior was the image each respondent maintained of God.

The study measured two ways in which people understood God: the degree to which they believed God was angry, and the degree to which God was directly engaged in human daily life. From this, the report sorted people's "God images" into four distinct categories:

- Authoritarian God (A)—High level of anger and high level of engagement
- Benevolent God (B)—Low level of anger and high level of engagement
- Critical God—High level of anger and low level of engagement
- Distant God—Low level of anger and low level of engagement

People's perceptions about God could predict more about their subsequent values and behavior than anything else measured, including ethnicity, age, gender, where they lived, or how much they earned. It was more powerful than education, political party, or even religious affiliation. Nearly one in three people surveyed—including atheists, agnostics, and religiously unaffiliated—maintained belief in an authoritarian God. This perception was the most prevalent by a full third over the second most common: the Distant God image. When we combine both the Authoritarian and the Critical God image people together (both of which perceive God as fundamentally angry), they make up nearly one-half of the entire population surveyed, or 47.4 percent.[1]

If we extrapolate this for the United States population overall, we can reasonably assume that just under 150 million people believe in an angry God. These people generally tend to be more faithful churchgoers, more generous givers, and more ardent students of Scripture than those with a more benign or benevolent understanding of God. The vast majority of churches are filled with people who maintain faith in this fundamentally angry God. They keep churches and denominations functioning, and they keep ministers employed.

In December 2007, the *Journal of Nervous & Mental Disease* released a study that found a person's belief systems had a significant impact on a brain function called the Evolutionary Threat Assessment System, or ETAS. This is the part of brain function that decides what threats there are in one's own environment, how great or imminent they are, and what, if any, action should be taken to avoid the threat. The study also found that a highly active ETAS can cause psychiatric disorders that are so severe, they become clinically pathological.[2]

In April 2013, an article by *Real Clear Science* cited another study done at Marymount Manhattan College that found:

...belief in a punitive God was significantly associated with an increase in social anxiety, paranoia, obsession, and compulsion. Conversely, belief in a benevolent God was associated with reductions in those four symptoms. Belief in an indifferent God was not linked to any symptoms.[3]

And according to the researchers themselves in the *Journal of Religious Health*, the image a person has of God not only affects how we feel about ourselves and life generally, but also has a significant effect on how we feel about daily events and how they affect us psychologically and emotionally:

...belief in a benevolent God inhibits threat assessments about the dangerousness of the world, thereby decreasing psychiatric symptoms (while) Belief in a punitive God...facilitates threat assessments that the world is dangerous and even that God poses a threat of harm, thereby increasing psychiatric symptomology.[4]

It's easy to cast a broad indictment over the whole of religion, or at least all of Christianity, for the perceived harm it has done and continues to do. And granted, if almost 150 million Americans believe in a fearsome God, there's plenty of blame to go around for pathologies brought on by religious practice. But it is important to note that, in both of the studies noted above, religious practices that focus on benevolent, loving images of God actually reduce these same pathologies, more so than in those maintaining no image of God at all. The following image lays out the effects graphically in a way that makes clear the profound difference in effects.[5]

Type of god
(What is the nature of God?)

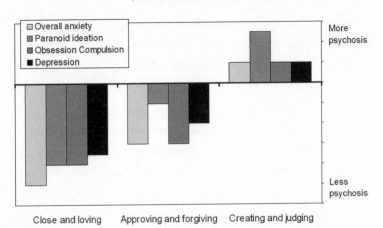

The *Journal on Healthcare Chaplaincy* suggested that these studies present strong evidence that " . . . activating a patient's own beliefs that God is loving and caring, and/or that God positively intervenes in one's life, would be a particularly potent method of reducing anxiety through these brain mechanisms."[6]

GOD, THE PANACEA

With all of the previously considered evidence, it is plain that Christianity in contemporary Western society presents somewhat of a paradox. The majority of our religious leaders present a God of judgment and anger that science has proven can lead to significant psychological damage. Within conventional evangelical Christianity, this God does not so much revel in the condemnation or suffering of humanity, but rather has established certain inalienable caveats and conditions that, if violated, result in dire and eternal consequences. For some, this sort of judgment is necessary in order for God to be righteous, or even fair, at least by human standards. But as for its effects on our present-day psyches, this places the entirety of the burden of our eternal fate in our hands. We're left wondering at every turn if we've passed God's muster or not. The fear is haunting and inescapable, as this God's grace is dependent on you, rather than the sovereignty of grace.

We are afraid of what we don't know. Uncertainty can be terrifying, and so we reflexively seek an antidote to that fear, even if it isn't reasonable or based on anything other than a desire for what we say or think to be the way it actually is. We are often poorly equipped to deal with people's present fears, struggles, and suffering in effective ways. Humans are afraid of death; much of Christianity has focused on what happens after we die. We obsess over the afterlife. But unless there is some special detour we have yet to discover, death is still an inevitable part of the equation. We aren't so good with this part.

Instead of dealing with the reality of death and the loss that accompanies it, we gloss over it with trite phrases that are supposed to make it all better.

"We can all rest assured that he's in a better place now."

"God needed another angel up in Heaven, so she had to answer the call when it came."

Death is hard, regardless of what's on the other side of it. It's particularly hard on those still living, given that they're dealing not just with the loss of a loved one, but they're also faced with the stark reality that life does eventually end. You're alive, and then, all of a sudden...gone.

Life, and death, would be so much easier if God would offer us a way around the hard stuff. But that's not what we get. And that, as we have already examined, is not what our faith promises. Instead, we're guided by the model presented by Jesus, a partner to help make the journey a little easier, not in the "Jesus is my best friend and keeps the bogeyman away" sense. Instead, there is comfort in knowing that the God we seek is not immune or indifferent to our suffering. Jesus gets it. He was afraid. The difference is that he didn't let that fear determine who he would be or what he would ultimately do.

The idea of a life absent of death and all of the hardship that comes along with it sounds pretty good, but it's also a life absent of real humanity. We are as defined, like it or not, by our scars as we are by our accomplishments and triumphs. And though we might yearn for a loophole, a way around the whole "death" thing, what we find in Scripture is that way *through*.

Consider the Twenty-Third Psalm, which is read at most funerals held in a Christian context. Nowhere in the Psalm does it say we don't have to go through the valley. We would prefer a shortcut, a way around the hard reality of dealing with our fears, a panacea that will make it all better. But in this Psalm, the darkness is still there, as is the evil all around. It is a dangerous journey, but one that can be made without fear because we are not alone. Yes, we still have to struggle, and life is replete with suffering. Rather than finding an easy way out, it's about summoning the courage to make it through.

The only real way out is through.

CHAPTER FOURTEEN

CARRYING EACH OTHER

THE CHRIST-LIKE VIRTUE OF COURAGE

Anyone who has gone to a Protestant church for any length of time probably knows what testimonial time in worship is all about. Basically, it's the time—usually after the sermon—when someone from the congregation goes to the front and shares how they became a Christian. The idea, at least in the churches where I grew up, was to convince the folks in the congregation who had not yet accepted Jesus into their hearts to do so, and/or to join the church as a member.

More often than not, the testimonial time became either a recruitment tool for Jesus, often steeped in fearsome stories about the consequences of not accepting him into your heart, or it was reduced down to someone sharing an excerpt from their daily meditation book or (after the invention of e-mail) the much-dreaded forwarded e-mail story.

I wasn't sure as a teenager why I disliked this part of worship so much. It was only later that I realized I didn't care for the fact that either it felt superficial and not particularly well thought-out, or it was strongly coercive and generally had some dire warning about the unpleasantness of Hell. I was already a Christian, and most weeks, there weren't any non-Christians in the church from what I could tell. And if I wanted to read *Guideposts*, I would have already been a subscriber; I didn't really want or need someone to read it to me.

So what was the point?

When Amy and I started Milagro Christian Church back in 2004, we were invested in a notion that Disciples of Christ proclaim, known as "the priesthood of all believers." As Amy always puts it in worship in simpler terms, we're all ministers and we all have a ministry. But how to empower people with their own authentic voice? How to help them discover what their ministry is? We wanted to involve people more actively in worship, but we both resisted the idea of testimonials, both because we were more interested in evangelism based on attraction rather than aggressive promotion, and also because both of us had similarly negative feelings about testimonial time in our past.

"I think it was a good idea," said Amy, "but something was lost in the execution. Instead of really sharing something about themselves, people fell into a habit of talking more about what they believed."

"Or they read something that just sounded good," I said, "but didn't have anything to do with their own lives at all. I think it's because we're afraid. The older we get, the more guarded we are about really sharing with each other.

"Hell, kids are better at sharing their lives than adults are. Just look at how much they love to do show-and-tell," I said.

And then it hit us: Why not do "show-and-tell" as a part of worship?

The instructions were simple. People were to bring something from home that helped them see God, and tell a story about it. No e-mail forwards. No scripts, and no altar calls. The stories should be about them, their lives, their mountain-top experiences in encountering the divine, as well as those points in life when God could not have seemed farther away. The experience of sharing was necessarily vulnerable for people. You could see some people's hands shaking as they took their turn telling their story. But as time went on, everyone in the congregation took part, from teenagers to the elders. Some shared stories about tattoos of crosses and the Virgin Mary, while others passed around family heirlooms from their grandmothers who read the Bible to them as children.

And each time another story was told, each time someone had the courage to lay a part of their lives bare as an offering to God and the rest of us present, our collective story became a little bit richer, a little stronger, a little more like the Body of Christ we'd been called to be.

THE COURAGE TO BE VULNERABLE

Brene Brown is a prominent author, speaker, and therapist, working with the concept of vulnerability. Her TED Talks, which resonate deeply with viewers, have received millions of hits online. One of the reasons that her message is so effective is that she herself practices and embodies vulnerability when she speaks to large groups. In modeling that kind of openness to people she doesn't even know, she gives even greater salience to her message.

In one of her talks, called "Listening to Shame," she takes on some critical misconceptions in our contemporary culture, which values autonomy and emotional stoicism:

...vulnerability is not weakness. And that myth is profoundly dangerous...Vulnerability is not weakness. I
define vulnerability as emotional risk, exposure, uncertainty. It fuels our daily lives. And I've come to the
belief—this is my twelfth year doing this research—
that vulnerability is our most accurate measurement of
courage: to be vulnerable, to let ourselves be seen, to
be honest...vulnerability is the birthplace of innovation, creativity and change...Adaptability to change is
all about vulnerability.[1]

Brown rightly points out that the vast majority of people in
our culture today equate vulnerability with weakness rather
than courage. However, in drawing such a false correlation,
and in trying to avoid what we believe is the weakness of vulnerability, we also cut ourselves off from what she calls "the
birthplace of innovation, creativity and change." She notes
that she has been flooded with requests to speak all over the
country following the popularity of her TED Talks. Invari-
ably, however, the institutions that invite her to present place
one caveat on her invitation: Do not talk about shame or vulnerability.

"What would you like me to talk about?" she asks them.
The answer: innovation, creativity, and change.

Former General Minister and President of the Christian
Church (Disciples of Christ) Dick Hamm says that the
mantra of a dying church is, "Ohmmm, but we've always
done it this way..." We're forever looking for the shortcut,
the loophole, the easy path to real, substantive change that
somehow allows us to circumvent the inevitably hard work
of vulnerability that comes along with actually changing. We

worry that our churches will come across as weak, that we will lose all credibility with the world around us.

As stated in the previous chapter, the only way out isn't around; the only way out is through. And if Brene Brown is right, the greatest act of courage that Christians can model—both as individuals and as larger institutions—is to be profoundly vulnerable, despite the risks. This includes being honest about our doubts, our fears, our ignorance. It requires us to share deeply of ourselves, offering our stories and even our lives to those who might reject us. It demands that we not live out our faith from behind the armor of doctrine, personal or religious certitude, or even actual physical force, but rather that we offer up humility, apology, and confession to our own wrongdoing at every necessary turn. We must believe so deeply in what we desire to share with others that we stake our very lives on it.

TEN DAYS, ONE HUNDRED MILES

The summer between our sixth- and seventh-grade years, every student at my school had to take part in a ten-day, one-hundred-mile hiking trip in the Pecos Mountains. All food, clothes, and bedding had to be carried and we had to learn how to make river water drinkable. We slept three to a tarp, with only two pieces of plastic above and below us for shelter. Every day, we'd make another ten-mile trek, set up camp, and then do it all over again.

The teachers involved in the trip were there mostly for emergencies. The guides, or *sherpas* as we called them, were upperclassmen who had gone through the camping experience themselves a few years earlier. They taught us how to navigate, how to build fires, and the best ways to cook over those fires.

Needless to say, we learned some valuable lessons in those few days. Most of us had assumed that the point of the trip was to go from being utterly dependent children to independent men. But that wasn't the point at all. Yes, there were points at which our personal limits were tested, and when each of us was capable of far more than we thought. But the true lesson in that ten-day trip was experiencing the value of *interdependence*.

We acquired this interdependence in moments when one of us faltered and the rest of us had to step in to pull some extra weight. We learned it when they sent us away to set up our tarps, not dictating how to do it or where to choose the right place for the night. We absorbed it in dividing our daily tasks, such as gathering wood, cleaning dishes, and decontaminating water. But more than anything else, we learned interdependence when we sat around the fire in the evening and shared stories.

The really hard stuff happened around the fire. Yes, we got blisters on our feet, and it was less than pleasant the night that our sleeping bags slid out from under the tarp, only to be covered by rain. We were hungry at times, uncomfortable, maybe even a little bit scared once or twice, but the thing that took the most courage was sharing with the other guys around the fire. And it's not so much that doing so made me individually stronger, but it sure as hell made us stronger as a group.

One thing we've lost out on more than anything else in our current culture is this element of sharing stories; we lack a common narrative. From prehistoric times until fairly recent memory, evenings and inclement days were spent huddled around a fire, whittling away at idle time by telling stories— some truer than others. But it's more than a matter of being out of practice. We often lack the courage to share deeply and vulnerably about our lives. We're taught instead to guard against such vulnerability, to present a façade that doesn't belie the imperfections, doubts, and insecurities just beneath the surface. But it is in summoning the courage to expose these very real parts of ourselves to one another through shared stories that we become more unified, coherent parts of a greater body.

Interdependence is about creating a whole that is stronger than the sum of its component parts, which is part of why Jesus says, "For where two or three are gathered in my name, there am I among them."[2] He's not talking about some magical alchemy that happens suddenly when people of a common faith come together; he knew it would be essential to our very survival. By gathering together, there are two different opportunities for courage: the courage to admit we need help from a brother or sister, and the courage to reach out when that same brother or sister is in need of us.

THE GOOD NEWS OF U2

Imagine if we all got to Heaven someday, only to find out it's more like a big, sprawling primitive fire pit than some spit-polished mansion with ivory gables and golden gates. Imagine, instead of a great banquet table, a smoldering campfire, a handful of pointy sticks, and half a dozen cans of Spam. Would we be disappointed? Shocked? Or maybe we would slow down, look around, and listen to the stories we'd hear around the fire, rather than allowing these log-scarred eyes to judge what we see for us. Maybe, instead of catering to us like some five-star restaurant, the afterlife offers the opportunity for us to serve one another, and to be served by those we care for in return.

There's a story about a man who dies and comes upon two rooms, one of which portrays Heaven, and the other, Hell. In both rooms, everyone is seated around a large, round table, with long sticks attached to their arms, and spoons on the end. In the center of the table is an enormous bowl of stew.

"I don't get it," the guy says. "It looks like Heaven and Hell are exactly the same."

"They appear to be," says his guide, "but look closer." In Hell, the people continue in vain to try to feed themselves, spilling the food they can't manage to get to their mouths because of the long sticks keeping them apart from nourishment. The only difference in Heaven is that everyone has figured out that they can feed one another. Everyone is satisfied, cared for by their brother.

It's vulnerable to allow yourself to be fed by someone else, be it literally, spiritually, or emotionally. As Brene Brown points out, it's countercultural to allow ourselves to be dependent on someone else, as we tend to equate this kind of interdependence with weakness. It also takes courage to feed one another, taking the risk that what we will offer will be rejected, or that once we are the ones being fed, there won't be enough to go around.

We're animals, but also creatures of spirit. We're connected by something bigger, wilder, and untamable when we choose to acknowledge it. Once the connection is made, it's a hard one to ignore. As the band U2 says in their song "One," we get to carry each other. But it takes courage on both sides to get anywhere.

Harry was one of my favorite guys at Milagro. He was in his eighties, body bent and fairly broken by decades of working in the local steel mill. And yet he had a light emanating from within him that defied his crumbling body. I still carry a little seed in my wallet that Harry gave me some ten years ago when he did show-and-tell at Milagro. It's a mustard seed, actually, which Jesus talks about in the Gospels. Harry, like most of us, had never seen a mustard seed before, let alone the plant it yields, at least until he went to Israel. They're actually so tiny, so seemingly insignificant, that it would be easy to mistake one for a speck of dust if you didn't know differently. But the trees they give life to are pretty remarkable, especially given their humble beginnings.

Harry was a simple guy. He worked with his hands in the steel mill all of his adult life. His body was small and fragile by the time I met him, and if you didn't know any better, you might think of him as unremarkable as the seeds he handed out during worship that day.

"I don't have a whole lot to say," said Harry. "I'm no preacher like Pastor Amy. But there have been times in my life, during the war, during hard times, when this was about as much faith as I could manage. But somehow, one way or another, it ended up being enough. And I thank God for that."

Harry died a few years ago, and Amy and I had the honor of conducting a small memorial service for him. I still have his seed, and I will never forget his story and the courage it took for him to share it.

CHAPTER FIFTEEN

TYRANNY OF THE UN-POSSESSED

THE CHRISTIAN SCANDAL OF ENVY

I was so excited to take my new Superman lunchbox to school, I could hardly stand it. I couldn't wait to show it off to all of my friends. And then I got there and saw Jason with his Teenage Mutant Ninja Turtles lunchbox, all the kids ogling it like it was the Holy Grail. Suddenly, my Superman lunchbox wasn't so great anymore. Sure, it was just as good a lunchbox as it had been before I got to school, but once I saw something better, it lost a lot of its value in my eyes.

The problem is, there's always something better out there. Our entire socioeconomic system is based on the presumption that you'll soon see something better than what you have, and that you'll do whatever you have to in order to get it. And once you get it, you'll start the cycle all over again.

Ideally, the Church would offer some antidote to such cycles of envy, but we can often be the worst offenders. One church covets another church's members. One church longs to have the biggest, nicest building. We covet the deacon's new car, while also silently judging him for not giving the money to charity instead. The practice of envy in our culture has become so normalized, it's practically a religious institution itself. Meanwhile, the Church—with a big C—is silent, if not complicit, in enabling such sickness to its own advantage, to build our numbers and acquire more in the name of "expanding our territory." There is power in envy, but it is a dark, insidious power we've come to welcome into our lives.

When the Church normalizes envy within its own inner sanctum, it sets the standard for us to do the same in the rest of our lives. If it's acceptable to speak covetously about this person's cushy job, that woman's extravagant car, or even the cross-town megachurch's gargantuan budget, it's easy to justify similar behavior the other 167 hours a week when we're not in worship.

There's also the matter of presenting an image of God that embodies this same envy. Growing up, I heard multiple claims that God is a jealous God who wanted us all to himself, and who seethed with envy every time we placed something in the way of an otherwise perfect relationship. It's as if God is a hapless, pining girlfriend whose heart we continue to step on over and over again. Basically, we're assholes. Plus, if we're created in the image of this God, it's only natural for us to act the same way. But this generates faith-based fear and narcissism. We're constantly letting God down, hurting God's feelings. Ironically, it's okay to be envious and jealous, so long as we're doing it for God.

FORGIVE US, FOR WE CARE NOT FOR WHAT WE HAVE

Though a close cousin of greed, envy is actually worse in its potential to do damage to relationships and larger communities. Greed is specific to our desire for more of, well...anything. It may or may not belong to someone else, but that is immaterial. Greed is all about getting what we want. But envy is personal. With envy, not only do we desire something we don't have; we long for the thing that another possesses, and we resent not having it. We begin to break them down in our hearts, bit by bit, justifying to ourselves why we should be enjoying such good fortune instead of them. By right, it should be ours, not theirs, and damn them for having the dumb luck to stumble into our well-earned good fortune!

Where greed is largely self-contained, envy is, in a strange and twisted sort of way, deeply relational. We long for what is possessed by the other. And more than that, we desire for them not to have it. We begin to justify why this is reasonable, too. We deserve what they have more than they do. What we have now is suddenly worthless, with all sense of value transferred to the un-possessed thing. And in the darkest recesses of envy lie the germinating seeds of violence, those inklings that, if we can't have the objects of our desire, then neither should the other. As Rene Girard says, we delight nearly as much in seeing them stripped of that thing as we would in having it ourselves.

In his book, *Deceit, Desire & the Novel*, Girard talks about the dynamics of what he calls "mimetic desire." The concept is that we create a sense of social order by imitating one another in various ways. We find someone—or more than one person—to identify with, and then we begin to assess what they do, what they have, and what is important to them. We begin to desire what they have, particularly those things that we deem are formative in making them who they are. But the desire goes beyond simple greed or covetousness; it actually gets personal:

...we envy first the one who possesses the object (this last one having finally a minor importance). And, in certain cases, we would feel more satisfaction in the fact that the *Other* does not possess the object, rather than to have it ourselves. Publicity, this hymn to the possession of objects, gives us to desire, not a product in its objective qualities but some people, *Others*, who desire this product or who seem gratified with its possession.[1]

Envy is a deeply rooted human impulse, firing off well below the intellectual conscious processes we might use to pretend we don't covet our neighbor's...you name it. It also knows no socioeconomic limits. But more important than our relationship with the object itself is, as Girard points out, our relationship with the individual (real or imagined) who possesses the object of our desire. This mimetic desire, though rooted in a kind of admiration for the other, allows our envy to consume us, reducing the one we seek to imitate in one moment to little more than fuel for resentment in the next.

One morning, on our way to church, I noticed a curious sequence of events, all of which happened in a matter of seconds. We drove by a bus stop, just down the street from our house, and the guy standing against the pole, waiting for his ride, swiveled his head slowly in time with our passing. Keep in mind that we drive a Prius, which is particularly unremarkable in a city like Portland. You could swing a dead cat and hit half a dozen. As this happened, I wondered to myself:

Who in the world would be jealous of a four-year-old Prius?

Apparently, the guy waiting in the cold for the bus.

Then we pulled up to the corner, next to a guy in his convertible Porsche, filling up at the gas station. Yes, it was cold, but if you wait for perfect weather to put the top down on your car in Portland, you'll enjoy the luxury for only about seventeen hours a year.

"Whoa," my eight-year-old son, Mattias, said and spun around in his seat, "did you see that? It's soooo awesome. I want a Porsche so bad!"

Now the adult in me, who fortunately had control of my mouth at the time, said something mature about being grateful for what we had, and asked him what he, a third-grader, would actually do with a hundred-thousand-dollar car, short of sitting in the driveway in it, hoping his classmates walked by to gawk. But the eight-year-old inside me wanted the Porsche just as badly as he did. In fact, I found myself sizing the driver up, guessing how he'd come into his money. *Probably works in some soulless cubicle all day*, I thought to myself, eyeing the candy apple red curves of the seductive car body. *This car brought to you by Enron!*

But the driver and his kid took no notice of us ogling his plush ride. It wasn't because they were so inured to people's adoration of their vulgar displays of wealth either (not like our perfectly practical and modest expressions of material necessity, mind you); it was because they were busy craning their necks to ogle the Harley idling noisily in front of us at the light. I might also mention that the guy on the chopper didn't notice their gazes because he was staring at the next car, looking up and down at the girl who was sitting next to a spectacled guy far less leather-clad and cool than he was.

My friend Brian Feille calls this phenomenon "the tyranny of the un-possessed." Though it's a poetic description, I think the degree of control such desire can have over our lives can hardly be overstated. We sense the deep burn of desire within ourselves, and then pin the blame for such emptiness on the absence of some external thing. *It's their fault I feel this way. They don't deserve what I want. Damn them for having what should rightly be mine!*

It is part of human behavior to invent narratives for other people's lives. We then compare these narratives to our real ones, and not surprisingly, our actual lives don't live up to the fantasy ones constructed for others. Then we search for differences between us and them, identifying those things about their lives that differ from ours, the means by which they must have achieved this perfect happiness we've invented for them only in our imaginations.

And then the voice of envy comes up from within us:

Who are they to have such happiness while I continue to struggle? What did they do to deserve a bigger, newer, shinier, faster (fill in the blank) than I have? If the world were just, that thing would be mine, not theirs. Their happiness should be mine!

A fictitious battle ensues, serving as judge, jury, and executioner, redistributing the material possessions and the concomitant happiness that certainly accompanies them. All of this happens in a split second, often somewhere deep within our unconscious brain. But it happens. It happens often, many times each day. We set the world correctly on its axis once again, tilting as it should, of course, in our well-deserved favor.

Henri Nouwen writes in his book *Making All Things New: An Invitation to the Spiritual Life* about this phenomenon that seems to keep us perpetually dissatisfied even in the most unspeakably beautiful moments. There must be something wrong with us; we've got to be crazy. It is a little nuts, to be honest, but the "good news" is that this brokenness is something we all share as participants in the greater human experience. Such imperfect joy is a testament, for better or worse, to the state of the human condition. Nouwen writes:

> ...there is no such thing as clear-cut pure joy, but that even in the most happy moments of our existence we sense a tinge of sadness. In every satisfaction, there is the fear of jealousy. Behind every smile, there is a tear. In every embrace, there is loneliness. In every friendship, distance. And in all forms of light, there is the knowledge of surrounding darkness.
>
> Joy and sadness are born at the same time, both arising from such deep places in your heart that you can't find words to capture your complex emotions. But this intimate experience in which every bit of life is touched by a bit of death can [make] us look forward in expectation to the day when our hearts will be filled with perfect joy, a joy that no one shall take away from us.[2]

The problem is, we're not easily satisfied with expectation alone. We want perfect joy now, on our own terms. We want to be able to invoke such joy by some means at our own immediate disposal. Such impatience is aggravated by the fantasies we construct about the already-present joy of others, diminishing our own joy by degrees.

Such a fundamentally tragic human flaw presents a tremendous marketing opportunity for those who choose to exploit it. And they do: retailers spend trillions of dollars a year painting the pictures of perfect joy, just out of our reach, yet conveniently attainable by purchasing their particular product or service. And it's not just a one-and-done system either. There's always a new version of the latest gadget just around the corner, and—surprise!—that item we purchased didn't give us that perfect sense of fulfillment we were hoping for after all.

Next time, we tell ourselves, *it will be different. I thought what I needed was this thing, but that was only until I saw THAT thing...*

It reminds me of the scene in the movie *The Jerk*, when Steve Martin is trying to leave the house in a dramatic flourish, but keeps getting bogged down with one thing or another that he can't leave without. "All I need is this lamp," he says, glancing around, "I don't need one other thing, not one... I need this... and the paddle game... and the chair... and the remote control... and the matches, for sure. And this. And that's all I need."

And we go on and on, throughout our lives, chasing our desires down an infinite rabbit hole while lining the pockets of companies feeding on our perpetual state of discontent. And as long as we remain complicit in the play, no matter how repetitive and transparent the script, the whole system keeps working. Some expressions of Christian theology, particularly those that emphasize personal salvation over all else, similarly exploit this deep-rooted envy we possess:

You are unhappy because you don't have Jesus in your heart. If you do what we tell you to do, that emptiness and darkness will all go away. Don't you want what I've got? My life is so much better than yours; you'd be a fool not to reach out and take what we're offering you.

Those of us in mainline and progressive churches who don't identify with this sort of theology, however, are equally guilty of envying the effectiveness of such a ministry. We in mainline Christian churches stand at arm's length and critique the wealthy TV evangelists and charismatic megachurch pastors, partly because we find their message objectionable, but also because we want what they have. It's easy to label such ministries as a farce, as some opportunistic distortion of Christ's Gospel, calling us to humility, sacrifice, and service. But most of us within the Church wish, deep down inside, that our congregations were bursting with people like theirs.

Rather than focusing on our own call to real justice, we wish our own kind of justice to rain down on other religious leaders we deem to be inferior, setting things as they should be, giving those who truly follow God's call what they deserve and exposing those we resent for what they believe they really are.

SPIT OUT THE POISON

I know it's maddening to see someone who we feel is less deserving get precisely the thing we want. It sets a toxin loose within us, coursing through us until it consumes our consciousness, diminishing what joy we may realize in the moment because of the envy that weighs so heavily over us.

Anne Lamott compares holding on to resentment to feeding yourself rat poison, and then waiting for the rat to die. If we allow ourselves to experience such a holy moment of clarity, we might see that the perceived injustice is not, in fact, where the problem lies; it's in the envy we attach to it.

All of us have an innate tendency to care how we compare to everyone else, though. It does matter, at least when we compare ourselves to someone who we believe has more (it seldom works the other way around). Christian leaders want their churches to be as full as the ones they condemn. They want to earn as much or be recognized as much as the peer they're sure doesn't do half the job. In this sense, they're no different—no less human—than the rest of us. Meanwhile, the communal well is poisoned, each of us drinking fervently from the brackish water while a spring of plenty continues to feed it.

I've often said that if we judged Jesus' time on earth based on the ways we determine our own success, he would be deemed a complete failure. He died alone; he was poor, humiliated, and suffering. No church. Nothing. He wouldn't have even had any Facebook friends. So why do we claim to be followers of Jesus, and yet continue to expect things to transpire on our own terms? If we didn't so desperately need someone to intervene, to help reset the entire paradigm, turning the whole system of value, justice, righteousness, and even success on its end, then why do we need the Gospel?

Leave it to us humans to keep poring over the texts, figuring if we look hard enough, or if we just want it badly enough, we'll find the magic loophole. After all, we deserve it, right? We long to find a way to bend circumstances and rules in our favor, whether within church or within a larger society. Surely there's a way to spin this "it's not all about you" Gospel thing so I can still get everything I want, right? How about if we focus on my neighbor, especially since he clearly has so much more than I do, and yet has done nothing more to deserve it?

Jesus didn't always get his own way either, and he certainly didn't get what he deserved. If he's our example, it seems wise to heed his own words when praying to God for the burden of crucifixion to pass him by:

Not my will, but yours, God, be done.[3]

CHAPTER SIXTEEN

WHAT LOVE BIRTHS

THE CHRIST-LIKE VIRTUE OF JUSTICE

We talk a lot about justice, both in church and else-where. Usually it's in the context of someone getting what we believe they deserve, like a criminal getting the electric chair or our nation winning a war with another country. Usually it's about vindication of our own beliefs, but this isn't the kind of justice Jesus talked about.

God's justice is different from the human understanding of justice. However, we, as imperfect human beings, can work to facilitate a God-like justice in the world. It takes a radical re-imagining of what we think of when we talk about justice.

When I was a kid in Sunday school, the word "justice" was usually used in the context of the book of Revelation or study of the Biblical prophets. Then, it evoked images of a great, terrible sword, severing the wicked from the righteous, or huge scales, holding the sum total of my life's choices in the balance, determining my eternal fate with each portentous swing.

Basically, justice scared the shit out of me. You wanted to be on the right side of it when the time came, because otherwise you were bound for Hell. You had one chance in this life to get it right, and when God's justice rained down, it would be as rivers of fire, fearsome horsemen trampling on the backs of the iniquitous, and the stench of carnage hanging in the air.

If we consider the life and ministry of Jesus, this kind of justice didn't seem to be the focus. He was much more concerned with how we treat one another and the lengths to which we would go to make sure our brothers and sisters had enough.

Conservative commentator Glenn Beck disparaged the notion of so-called social justice, but is there really any other kind? Justice doesn't exist in a vacuum; it requires community to be realized. And though we are obsessed with fairness and getting what we deserve, true justice is actually unfair by our standards. My understanding of justice is a healing of all the divisions we have created among us, be they divisions of class, race, orientation, ideology, age, or political party. In my image of justice, God tears down the silos in which we store up our surpluses and endeavor to protect that which is ours. It is the great leveling of the so-called playing field. No longer will we be valued based on human metrics, but rather by the universal, liberating power of grace. It may not seem fair to someone who has worked hard to be a good Christian, or a successful businessperson or a well-known author, but such superficial values fall short of one who benefits from unearned grace.

No one wants to believe in a God that is unfair, but if fairness and justice actually stand in opposition to each other, I'd prefer to be in the graces of a just God, rather than a fair one. God help me if I get all I have coming to me.

BOMBS IN BOSTON

"I heard someone dropped a bomb on Boston," said Mattias over breakfast while I scrolled through the breaking news reports.

"Not exactly," I said. "It was two guys. Two brothers who came from Russia. They dropped homemade bombs by the finish line of the marathon."

"Why?" he asked.

"I really don't know."

"Maybe they were angry about something, and they didn't know how to talk about their feelings."

"Maybe so." I nodded.

"Did they hurt people?"

"A lot of people," I said. "More than a hundred."

"And they didn't do anything to deserve that."

"No," I said, "they didn't."

"Did they kill anyone?"

"Three people," I said, hoping his questions would stop, while knowing full well they wouldn't.

"Who died, Dad?"

"Well," I sighed, "a young woman who was a college student, and a boy..." I watched his face fall and his mouth go slack. We sat in silence for at least a minute, though it felt like hours.

"That's really terrible," he whispered. I nodded in silence. "That kid didn't do anything."

"It's pretty messed up," I said. Then his face began to harden.

"If I saw those guys"—he raised his voice—"I would take a cinder block and..." His voice trailed off as he realized the hopelessness of trying to make anything right out of such chaos, such senseless violence.

"I know, buddy. It's hard to understand. And it's okay to have feelings about it."

"I hope they feel really bad about what they did," he scowled. Amy helped slip his backpack over his shoulders as we scooted him toward the front door. He was late for school. "Oh, and don't forget to bring cupcakes by the school today for the carnival," he said. "Store-bought only. School rules."

"All right, buddy. Try to hustle so you won't get a tardy slip."

Store-bought cupcakes. Because God knows what someone might do to homemade treats for elementary school kids.

God knows what someone might do.

BENDING THE ARC OF HISTORY

If Jesus is, in fact, the example to which we look for the model of justice, let's consider for a moment the point at which he is near death on the cross. He was abandoned by all who claimed to love him, and he was taunted and tortured by figures of authority. All of this was because he refused to abandon his message of radical, empire-shaking love that stood firm in the face of any force, fear, or hate intent on its destruction.

Talk about unfair.

And in the culminating moment, when Jesus would be justified in condemning those who fell so woefully short, he calls out to God on their behalf:

Father, forgive them, for they know not what they do.

We will never understand this act of total selflessness in our lifetime. When I read about Jesus' act of sacrifice, I whisper a sigh of relief that God is God, and I am not. I can't even look at my neighbor's car, home, job, etc., and not think about myself, let alone keep others at the center of my heart.

We can reorient ourselves toward Jesus' example of sacrifice when we've lost our way, and we can take small, tentative steps in that direction day after day, even if we stumble and falter.

It is the summit toward which the arc of history bends. It is "Thy kingdom come." And fortunately for all of us, it's based on a notion of love and grace whose scope transcends any human notion of fairness.

LOVE GREATER THAN "OTHER"

Jeffrey Toobin's book about the United States Supreme Court called *The Nine*, is fascinating. He identifies how the Supreme Court is set apart from the other two branches of government, beholden to neither when making decisions. Some partisanship is represented in the role, but once elected, the court justices can rule however they see fit for as long as they choose to serve.

As autonomous as they are in their authority, the justices hardly live in a vacuum. *TIME* magazine published a piece about Justice Anthony Kennedy, a critical swing vote in the court. One relationship in Kennedy's life may have done more for gay rights in America than many better-known movements for equality throughout our history.

Kennedy was good friends with Gordon Schaber, the dean of his law school, and Schaber became a mentor for the young Kennedy. Over time, it became clear that Schaber was living an emotionally difficult secret life as a closeted gay man. Since he had such a profound respect and love for this man, the relationship arguably deepened Kennedy's understanding of human sexuality.

Professor J. Clark Kelso, from the same McGeorge School of Law, says in the article, "I don't see how it [the relationship between Kennedy and Schaber] could not have had some impact on Kennedy's later rulings on gay rights."

Though traditionally more conservative when it comes to his votes on so-called social issues, Kennedy has been a firm supporter of gay rights, as the article notes. So despite Kennedy's rigorous intellect, tireless work ethic, and steadfast commitment to judicial integrity, that one relationship likely has had more impact on his rulings as a key swing vote on the Supreme Court than anything else. There's a place in our culture—and indeed, in the Church—for speaking out for what we believe. Advocating at the legislative level for equality is important. But real, substantive change takes place in one mind, one heart, one relationship, and one person at a time.

It is interesting that the modern handshake came from warfare. Showing one's open right hand was a way of demonstrating one was unarmed. In fact, men did not use to grab hands, rather they grabbed hold of each other's forearms, another subtle gesture to ensure one's potential adversary was harmless. But it also pushed people into physical contact with each other, forcing them to acknowledge one another's humanity. That personal contact is perhaps our most powerful weapon in waging peace.

Throwing stones at one another from a safe distance is

easy. It's an altogether different matter to be put in the vulnerable position of face-to-face contact with something or someone that makes us uncomfortable. But where we come together as a community—not from deeply entrenched bunkers or behind fortified walls—God meets us there, and beautiful things happen.

We're called to tear the veils of division in two, erasing the boundaries that separate, not in some feebly color-blind attempt at political correctness, but in actually seeking out and summoning forth the God we believe dwells within each of us.

Jesus says that whatever we do to the least of these, we do to him, but consider that in a more literal way than we tend to think of it. It wasn't just some nice metaphor to get us to be kind to each other. By living lives of self-gratification built on inherently violent and oppressive mechanisms, we're crucifying the innocent, over and over again. Justice is realized only when we act on this faith in an utterly leveling, equalizing grace that destroys all systems of inequity, oppression, and exploitation. It's not a kingdom vision if we simply sit by and pray for God to bring it to us; we are to be the agents of this grace in a world that has normalized, and even celebrates, "self over other."

Though Jesus' death was clearly unjust, it was also inevitable. This isn't to say that it was necessary (as some Christians will claim) in order to make good on our debt of sin; there's an important difference. It was inevitable not because God required it, but because of how we have historically responded to people when we cannot bear their truths: we kill them.

Jesus was a fitting scapegoat on multiple levels. He clearly represented a threat to the Roman social system by which they maintained power and order. He let down his own followers by not responding to "Hosanna, save us" in the way they had hoped and expected. Although his followers were disheartened by his refusal to employ force or violence to free them of the Roman occupation, it is this very shift of paradigm—Jesus' refusal to operate within the system of existing societal norms, to use force to overthrow force, but rather to hold fast to the incorruptible faith that God's boundary-defying love cannot be beaten out of a man, a nation, or a community of faith—that threatened the Roman Empire. He had to be extinguished.

Jesus died because he refused to abandon radical love in exchange for fear. He died because humanity chose, despite his example, to cling to fear. And the cost of such fear is death, indeed. It has been so since the beginning of recorded history, and it continues to be today. Fear leads to violence; violence, to death. And all of it is predicated on our own less-than-Christ-like obfuscation of justice.

Jesus spoke throughout his ministry of such "unfair" types of justice—for example, when he tells the story of the Prodigal Son, who gets far more than he deserves, while the good son is relegated to the background. There's the parable of the laborers, in which all are paid the same, no matter how much they worked. Who among us would consider that fair treatment?

And yet this is how Jesus describes God's justice.

The full embodiment of the kind of justice Jesus talks about is what brought the great temple in Jerusalem to rubble. Some saw this as a catastrophe at the time, but actually it was a point of in-breaking of God's kingdom. Jesus prophesied the destruction of the temple not because he hated religion part and parcel, but because those within the temple system had come to value the system itself more than the justice it was intended to help realize in the world. It was a brilliant, gold-covered monument that originally was meant to be a tribute to God, but which had become a monument to the humanity of those who controlled it. The walls had become barriers of class and status, even delineating the boundary of God's grace. And when the walls, boundaries, and other efforts to maintain "otherness" fall away, we are left together, face-to-face, confronted with mirrors that reflect that which we fear most about our own selves.

We might seek to strike out and kill it, to shatter the image that bears such undeniable evidence of our own injustice, our own brokenness. We long to maintain the illusion of wholeness, of sovereignty that can only be maintained from behind high walls, in a climate-controlled reality into which no dissent, no difference, no outsider can enter in to defile the sanctuary of our own self-righteousness.

And we call this justice because it suits us.

But real justice is terrifying because it means we must make ourselves vulnerable to one another's suffering. It is the fear of such shared suffering that keeps us from fully realizing one another's joy, too. A community unified by deep compassion divides its sorrows among the many, while multiplying the infinitely renewable resource of joy. We seek to contain it, to possess it, for fear of losing it altogether. And in doing so, we snuff out the flame, starving it of the oxygen needed to exist. We kill the thing we claim to want.

Which is why we need the life, the ministry, and even the death of Jesus to help point the way, once again, every day we draw breath. We need it to remind us to offer up all of who we are and what we have to those who we don't even deem worthy of it. We are reoriented when we are inclined to justify ourselves and our way of life toward a vision of God's kingdom that we know looks far different. We do not rest while others suffer, while they hunger, are exploited by our neighbor, or even by our own life choices. Everything else in life pales in comparison to the ceaseless effort to realize this justice. Right here. Right now.

Justice is realized when the hungry are fed, when the lonely are comforted, when the sick are made well, and when we make right the imbalances of the world that facilitate oppression, violence, and disparity. It isn't something issued with a gavel from behind a courtroom desk; it's something striven for, yet never entirely reached.

This kind of justice feels messy, because there's always more to be done. Some people take Jesus' claim that we will always have the poor with us as an excuse to shrug our shoulders and do nothing. But what if it was an implicit command to be tireless in our efforts to seek justice? What if he really meant all that stuff about loving with everything we have and every part of who we are?

And what might the world look like if we did? I can only imagine.

CHAPTER SEVENTEEN

WHICH SIDE OF HISTORY?

WHAT'S LEFT? CAN WE FIX IT? DO WE CARE?

The Christian faith has been through many cycles in the past two thousand years. There was a time when Christianity was still a fledgling resistance movement, meeting in secret in homes around Thessalonica, Galatia, and Rome, when it seemed the entire faith might not make it. Paul wrote letters of instruction, warning, praise, and guidance to those bands of faithful Christians, hoping to offer them what they needed, long enough to endure the oppression of the Roman Empire, which was intent on squashing the rebellious insurgent network.

Of course, we know that many of those letters make up much of the New Testament and we continue to read, debate, and draw conclusions from its wisdom today. However, Paul was addressing the immediate needs of those before him, reaching out to them in the spirit that had so dramatically transformed his life.

He had no idea that an emperor named Constantine would, one day, claim Christianity as the state religion of the Roman Empire, nor could he have predicted the work of Gregory of Nyssa and his council of leaders, who formulated what we now know as our Bible. It would have been impossible to predict, at the beginning of the fledgling Christian movement, the establishment of the Catholic Church in the heart of the land that had once endeavored to wipe the Christian faith from the annals of history. Nor would Paul have had any inkling that a man named Martin Luther would nail his ninety-five theses to the door of the Catholic Church in Wittenberg. In fact, I doubt Luther himself could have known that, in that moment, he had given birth to what we now call the Protestant Reformation.

Neither of them could have known how many lives would be changed for the better, or how many millions would be sacrificed in the name of the God they both claimed to love and serve. If he were here today, imagine what Paul would think of our fretting over the fractious nature of our denominational structures, arguing over doctrine and dogma, seeking feverishly to prop up our decaying institutions, which now stand in many ways as relics of a faith that has long since outgrown them. I expect it would be sufficient to make him lose his lunch.

Likewise, we can't imagine what the Christian faith might look like a thousand years from now. We are too concerned about being right *right now*, and about propping up teetering power structures, to even reflect on something so much greater and more enduring than our own lives and churches.

It's not about us. It never was. But success and power have a nefarious tendency to intoxicate those whom they inhabit, convincing them that such good fortune is at least well deserved, if not divinely ordained. Meanwhile, people have turned away by the millions, disenchanted and disenfranchised by the hypocrisy, the infighting, and the apparent self-serving nature of organized religion. Have they turned their backs on God altogether? Some have, perhaps. But for the most part, people don't hold the ills of humanity against their creator.

In trying to make sense of our faith, God, and the Bible in ways that feel satisfying and resolved, we risk missing the greatest gifts the Christian faith can offer us. We get so caught up in trying to draw lines of judgment around our society, trying to predict the final outcomes of our lives, in a sense, trying to do the work of God.

Meanwhile, we lose the mystery in our desperate attempts to make sense of it all. We have forfeited the liberation of mysticism for the desperate—but futile—pursuit of certainty. We seek God within our doctrines, laws, and institutional structures, but the God revealed by Christ was in the boundary-smashing margins, in unanswerable questions, enigmatic parables, in sighs too deep for words.

God finds a way to reach people again, to kindle the spark of longing within them, setting them out on a new path, seeking new understandings of who they are, where they come from, and why they are here. We long for authentic community, to feel as if we matter, belong, make a difference. There's something inherent in human nature that causes us to yearn for deeper meaning in our lives, in spite of the layers of scar tissue built up over years of trauma, doubt, or heartbreak. The new conversations taking place within the Church do not sound very familiar to those who adhere to traditional structures, and as such, may be labeled as heresy or apostasy.

The movement has, once again, wriggled free from the confining grip of history that seemed intent on conforming

God into humanity's own image. Christianity is attracting a more diverse crowd than ever before. Some speak with tongues unfamiliar to their predecessors. They wear clothing and decorate their bodies in ways that don't befit the traditional systems of worship, piety, and discipleship. They are freaks, outcasts, searching on the fringes for a firm foothold on which to plant themselves. They long for grounding, while also being wary of the history from which they long to distinguish themselves.

Are we in the midst of another great spiritual revolution? Have we embarked on what will be known hereafter as the Third Great Awakening? Only history gets to decide where the present circumstances fit within the larger conversation. We are participating in a phenomenon whose ultimate impact is yet to be fully determined. What remains after our passing is anyone's guess.

On the Verge of Mystery

The Christian faith is "on the verge of something new and uncertain." Attitudes toward organized religion are rapidly changing in Western culture. Church attendance is in sharp decline across the board for nearly all Protestant denominations, as well as for the Catholic Church. People are walking away from Christianity in record numbers, and those who are sticking around are reframing the story in ways that don't seem to fit the old formulas.

The Christian Church is going through both an identity crisis and a credibility crisis as a result of its own behavior, as well as overall social trends. These two factors combined have generated a seismic shift in the ways people engage and understand religion in their lives and culture. As yet, the new, alternative ways aren't entirely defined.

It has become evident that an alternate way of viewing the Christian faith in the twenty-first century Western world does not conform to any predictable formula. We've been making bold claims about end-times for centuries now, to the point that much of the world has stopped paying attention. But imagine if the Christian narrative read more like Kerouac's *On the Road* and less like a *Die Hard* movie. Consider what would be left of our faith if the lines between the good guys and bad guys were blurred, or even nonexistent. What if we spent less time and energy worrying about the conclusion of the story, and instead decided to focus on recognizing the present moment—Thy kingdom come, already here and now, in our midst. Let's focus more on baring our own souls to one another, exposing our deepest longing, our fear, our hope, and the less-than-perfect parts of who we are, rather than focusing so intently on saving the souls of others.

Our faith can still remain at the core of who we are, even after letting go of and possibly even unlearning the old ways. It is possible to find a place in this rapidly changing world where the life and message offered by Jesus still touches lives, communities, even nations, in transforming and radical ways. But rather than being Christ to the world as we've been called, the Church as we know it has become one of the stumbling blocks to achieving such a vision. This has to change.

We've fallen short of what Jesus is calling us toward, and now we've got to figure out how we might get back on the path of this Christ-inspired vision. This is the meaning we seek in the story of Christianity.

In order to find that, we—like Kerouac, Ginsberg, and

their fellow travelers—have to give ourselves over to the journey at hand. Where we will end up, both individually and collectively, is clouded in deep mystery, but also met with hopeful anticipation if we allow it. Jesus gave us permission to let go of such concerns. He reminded his followers not to focus on when he would return or how all of the prophets' visions would be fulfilled[1] or even who held the status of greatest favor with God.

All of these buildings, these institutions, these human-made constructs will decay and die, he reminds us.[2] So why cling so tightly to them? Let the institutions serve their purpose when, how, and if they can. However, if we assess Christ's presence and movement in our world based on "butts and bucks" metrics—the numbers of people in the Sunday pews and dollars in the offering plate—we've missed the real meaning of the story.

SIGNS OF LIFE

When I first met Phil, I made a lot of assumptions about him, most of which were wrong. He's an unassuming, thin, bespectacled white guy with a face that belongs on a twelve-year-old. He is soft-spoken, preppy, leads a modest church in Missouri, and uses phrases like "goodness knows" and "for gosh sakes" a lot.

I gave him the nickname "Huckleberry" because he's just such an "aw, shucks" kind of guy, but we all know how deceptive appearances can be. He has one of the sharpest intellects and also the driest sense of humor of anyone I know, which takes you particularly off guard because of how he looks. But he knows exactly who he is and what he's doing.

We first met at an event in the South where I had been asked to speak. I knew within a few minutes of chatting over lunch that we would be good friends. He later brought me out to his church to speak, and it was one of the most enjoyable events I've experienced. The energy of anticipation, radical openness, and a hunger for deeper knowledge was thick in the air. I felt joy for the church body's welcoming attitude, and for their fervent desire to share that same feeling with others they hadn't yet met.

That's a rare trait in a lot of congregations. Either the community is clinging to life, desperately longing for an infusion of bodies and pledges to keep an aging system alive, or they love what they have so much that they fear sharing it too openly, in case others might come in and change things. But to have something you value so much that you can't help sharing it is truly inspired, and such inspiration generally comes from equally inspired leadership.

Their church in Springfield isn't perfect, but what they're doing matters. They've planted themselves in the middle of a community that sits comfortably in the heart of the Bible Belt. Phil readily acknowledges his own progressive leanings, but he also enjoys admitting that he has more than a handful of Republicans in the chairs on Sunday mornings. Next to them will be bleeding heart former hippies, skeptical intellectuals, college students on the fringes of faith, former Catholics, agnostics, and others who have no particular idea what they believe.

But they all fit together in some strangely beautiful way. They need and love one another. That, to me, is a glimpse of the kingdom of God.

WHAT'S LEFT? CAN WE FIX IT? DO WE CARE?

As a youngster, I heard quite a bit about something in Scripture called the Refiner's Fire. From Genesis through Revelation, there are dozens of direct and implied references to this kind of spiritual refining fire in our midst.[3] I tended to equate these verses with fear back then, as if the Refiner's Fire was something that would spare the righteous and incinerate the undeserving. It was, in some ways, synonymous with our understanding of Hell.

Today, I have come to welcome a refining fire in my own life, as I think we should within the larger Christian Church. Yes, some, if not all, of what we call "Christianity" is changing. Truly, much of it needs to, to be burned away, in order to make room for new life. Some argue that Jesus came to abolish religion, citing his conspicuous absence from the temple during much of his ministry, along with his prophecies of the temple's destruction, and his castigation of the self-serving moneylenders within the sacred walls. Others contest that he came principally to build the Church as the manifestation of his still-living body among us.

In both cases, we tend to see the Jesus that we want to find. But while building up the ongoing Christian body on the one hand through empowerment of his disciples to carry on his Gospel work, he also welcomed the Refiner's Fire. He saw it not as a force of destruction, but a fire of perfection, consuming what does not give life, leaving space for the things that really matter to flourish.

So what's left? With regard to the religious institutions, we're left with an infrastructure that once served a purpose whose time has now largely passed. This is not to say that we don't need set-aside spaces in our lives, sanctuaries to which we can retreat from the insistence of daily life to reconnect with ourselves and the Holy. But the model on which the Church of sixty years ago currently exists presumes much about our culture that isn't relevant any longer. We change jobs more often, relocate across the country, commute to work from twenty miles away, or even work from home. The Church isn't at the center of our cultural context anymore; communities are far more mobile and diverse than only two generations ago.

So we're left both with an institution that was built to accommodate a culture that has changed radically around it, as well as an administrative infrastructure that was created to support far more people and Church buildings than it now sustains. Much of this necessarily should be cleared away, dramatically reformed into something new, or even plowed back into the earth, so to speak, to help yield whatever will come next. Otherwise, we're stewards of very costly, but generally culturally irrelevant, headstones for a time now gone.

Fortunately, this speaks little to what is left of the Christian faith itself. In a culture desperately searching for authenticity, meaning, grounding, and connection, the Gospel message resonates on a level far deeper than intellectual knowing or even emotional connection. When faced with it, free of the layers of religious mandates, distortions, and quibbling, there is a truth within Jesus' life and teaching that is compelling and attractive. This is revealed best through our own lives, transformed by the Gospel as well, shining a brilliant light on what it is we believe is worth living, and perhaps even dying, for.

No one wants to live or die for the sake of a building, the

size of a congregation, or a list of doctrines. But for the kind of love and reconciling justice that brings a Christ-inspired kingdom of God to us, here on earth, there's nothing else more worth our time.

There is no question that Christianity as a religion has been in need of a refining fire for some time, and it's not surprising that the idea is met with some fear and self-preserving instinct. But if we truly trust that it is a fire of perfection and not consumption, what do we have to fear?

There is still much burning away to be done. And rather than dousing the flames, fearful that they will burn up the Church we have built, we should invite them in, much like the Pentecostal fires that settled above the heads of the disciples at the very moment this Christian movement was born in earnest. We may lose some churches and jobs we have come to depend on, but the followers of Christ are not called to focus on sustaining these things; that was never our calling. This is why Jesus reminds us that the temple—and even the whole of Jerusalem—will fall.

Don't cling too tightly to that which will, like you, yield to ash and dust.[4]

The Church as we as we know it is only so much ash and dust, held together by our own hopes and desires. But it can still be used toward the purposes laid out in the Gospel. Just like Jesus didn't need a church or a denomination behind him to live out his call, neither do we.

To me, the answer is found in Paul's letter to the new Christians in Rome. Ironically, Paul is credited more than anyone with founding the Church as we know it, but in his letter to the early Christian Church in Rome (Romans 8:1–17), he is clear about where our trust and our priorities

should lie. Following are some choice excerpts from that incredibly moving passage:

> A new power is in operation. The Spirit of life in Christ,
> like a strong wind, has magnificently cleared the air...
> In his Son, Jesus, [God] personally took on the human
> condition, entered the disordered mess of struggling hu-
> manity in order to set it right once and for all. The
> law code, weakened as it always was by fractured hu-
> man nature, could never have done that. The law always
> ended up being used as a Band-Aid on sin instead of a
> deep healing of it.
>
> So don't you see that we don't owe this old do-it-
> yourself life one red cent? There's nothing in it for us,
> nothing at all. The best thing to do is give it a decent
> burial and get on with your new life. God's Spirit beck-
> ons. There are things to do and places to go!
>
> This resurrection life you received from God is not
> a timid, grave-tending life. It's adventurously expectant,
> greeting God with a childlike "What's next, Papa?"[5]

We've done enough Christian grave tending. In the mean-
time, there is deliverance from such a thankless existence, if
only we're willing to accept it. It requires a release of expectations, of desire, and a surrendering of our fear that,
without our careful watch, God cannot survive in the world.
But this cleansing—this refining fire—is the liberation that
we long for at the core of our being, even as it scares us to
admit it.

What will go away, or what has already been burned off
by the refining fire, is not worth fixing or saving. This in-

cludes not only our aging and empty buildings, but also the legalistic, nit-picking ideologies and human-made divisions that should be cast into the fire. It is the stuff of death, and it's best left in the grave where it belongs. As for what's left once the refinement is through, it only requires, as Paul says, the faithful, hopeful anticipation of "What's next?" So the question of whether we can fix what we perceive to be broken in the Christian faith is less important than our need to accept and surrender that which is not life-giving. What lies at the heart of the Gospel is incorruptible and never needed perfecting by our hands, and certainly is more enduring than the Church ever will be. The truths within the life and ministry of Jesus will remain, regardless of our future as a religion. The essence of the stories is inscribed within us, even if some of the parables fade from our memories. As cultivators of this Gospel truth, we now need to awaken and stir the passion and desire to explore what already resides within each of us, rather than focusing on maintenance of an institution that will infuse the Gospel into us from the outside in.

One question remains: Do we care? It depends on who the "we" is that we're talking about. If we're asking if Christians—those within the institutional Church—care about something other than maintenance of their infrastructure and preservation of their current ways of life, that is a hotly debated matter, tossed back and forth over Church boardroom tables and from the pulpit on Sunday morning. Having done a great deal of work in the area of congregational transformation, I always put a simple question to the congregations I visit that helps clarify, in no uncertain terms, where their priorities lie:

If you could completely realize the mission of this congregation today, here and now, but in order to do it, you'd have to close the doors of this church and walk away forever, would you do it?

In a few instances, the answer is "no," in which case we are serving a human-made institution before we are serving the call of the Gospel. Simply put, this is idolatry and there is little help for such a congregation unless they are willing to change. Most other times, the answer is "yes." If it is an earnest, heartfelt "yes," that the institution is serving the mission, this is a healthy church whose priorities are in proper order. The survival of the organization itself will always come in a distant second to living out the commands of Jesus to love with all we have and all that we are, regardless of the cost.

Sadly, there are times when churches can't even begin to answer the question, namely because they lack any clearly defined mission beyond the preservation of traditions and an aging building. In these cases, the nonanswer speaks more profoundly than any explicit answer could. We tend to get caught up in a pattern of survival, hardly stopping to think about why we do it. This is not an exclusive phenomenon of churches either. I've met plenty of people in lifeless marriages who admit that there is no love in the relationship. And yet when asked why they persist, they tend to respond with a shrug and a few words of resignation, like, "It's just what we do."

So far, this has only addressed those within the Christian community, actively engaged in religious practice. And as the title of this book points out, this is a shrinking group throughout most of the Western world. But most people out-side the Church or beyond religion don't particularly care what happens to Christianity as we know it. With the grow-ing 'nones' and the frequency with which others are actively leaving the faith, it seems to be a nonissue. That can, how-ever, be deceptive. It is not necessarily that they lack the persistent longing for truth, meaning, community, hope, and a truly sustaining kind of love that holds the world together. They just don't see organized religion as the best or only means by which to engage those questions in the most mean-ingful way.

Even the most passionate atheist tends to hold up the virtues outlined throughout this book as central to our social order, and to leading a fulfilling life of substance. Christians expose their own hubris when they suggest that, because someone does not conform to their understanding of what it means to be a "Christian," they cannot possibly be Christ-like. There are plenty within religious Christianity who fall well short of the model set out for us by Jesus, while there are many beyond the Christian faith who more consistently live out what Jesus calls us to do and be. Personally, I con-sider the latter more of a Christian than the former. And in that sense, there are many in the world who bear the likeness and heart of Christ, but to which some Christians are blind because of dogmatic, cultural, or ideological differences. To answer "Do we care?" we must decide what we (religious Christians) care more about: seeing more people find ways to bear the heart and likeness of Christ in the world, wherever they are and however they identify themselves, or getting more names on a list, more players on our team, to feel vali-dated that our way is the one and only way.

It is counterproductive that we continue to debate the things we may never agree on, rather than beginning with common virtues and those soul-stirring questions that seem to be so inherent in the universal human condition. Those conversations are crucial to understanding how we move forward in determining much of the course of Christian community and practice.

ARE WE READY?

Phil had a pretty remarkable experience in 2012 that he didn't see coming. As a progressive religious leader in a predominantly conservative town, he feels it's incumbent to speak out *as a Christian* on issues about which most people assume all Christians are one-sided. In this particular case, there was a debate in the city council about equality of rights for gay and lesbian people. Phil framed his argument in the way most would expect a good Christian pastor to do. He spoke of the non-Biblical homosexual lifestyle and held up the virtues of Biblical marriage.

And then he paused, holding an awkward silence for a moment as he shuffled his papers. Following was the conclusion of his speech:

> You see, "The right of [segregation...uh, hold on...the right of segregation] is clearly established by the Holy Scriptures, both by precept and example."
>
> Oh wait, I'm sorry [more awkward fumbling], I brought the wrong notes. I borrowed my argument from the wrong century. It turns out what I've been reading to you are quotes from white preachers from

times like the 1950s and 60s in support of things like racial segregation and interracial marriage. All I have done is taken out phrases like "racial integration" and substituted them with phrases like "gay rights."

I guess the arguments I've been hearing around Springfield lately sounded so similar to these that I got them confused. I hope you won't make the same mistake. I hope you'll consider which side of history you wish to stand on.[6]

The city council, like many around the country, allows cameras into their chambers during public meetings. That particular night, a local news station happened to be filming the proceedings, and they put Phil's speech, along with several others, on their website. A few people watched it, but nothing changed. This was in August 2012. By the middle of October, a news aggregator site called Gawker picked up the story and shared the video on its website. Within forty-eight hours, the video of Phil's speech had gone viral, receiving more than 2.5 million views. Within a few months, it had neared 4 million views. The Gawker story posted on a Friday, and by Monday, Phil had producers from the *Today* show, *NBC Nightly News*, *The Ellen DeGeneres Show*, and scores of others seeking him out, panting for exclusive interviews and overwhelming his tiny church staff with e-mails and phone calls.

I asked Phil why it was that his speech exploded like it did, from apparently out of nowhere.

"As for why Gawker decided to pick it up when they did," he says, "I have no idea. But I think the reason the thing went viral was because of where we are in history in our culture.

We're ready to have this conversation. We're ready to look at ourselves and ask why it is that the rights of some people are in any way different than the rights of those seeking equality back in the sixties."

GET ON THE BUS

I have not spoken with my dad in over six years, so when my aunt Sandra called me and told me she and my uncle Jim were coming to Portland for a real estate conference, I was more than a little bit anxious. I hadn't, after all, seen them or any other member of my dad's side of the family since my wedding in the summer of 2000. I imagined sitting awkwardly around the dining room table, speaking indirectly about the most obviously absent person in the room, but I wanted them to know my children so we invited them for a meal.

As is often the case, my worries far exceeded reality. They were gracious, loving, and adored my kids just like nieces and nephews should be adored. We shared wine, laughed, caught up, and spun a few stories over baked penne and spinach salad.

"Where do you live?" Mattias asked.

"Montgomery, Alabama," said Sandra. "Do you know where that is?" He shook his head. "It's in the old South, where Martin Luther King Jr. used to live."

"Oh," said Mattias, his face brightening, "I know about him. He preached about equality for African-Americans."

"That's right," said Sandra. "And have you heard of Rosa Parks?"

"I think so, but I'm not sure."

"She was African-American," said Sandra, "and back then, people with black skin had to sit behind a line drawn across the floor in the back part of the bus."

"No way!"

"Yep," she said, "they would get on in front, pay their money, and then they'd have to get back off the bus, walk to the door in back, and get on back there, behind the line."

"That's just terrible," Mattias said, incredulous.

"The thing is, if a white person got on the bus and didn't have anywhere to sit in front, the black people had to get up and give their seats to the white passengers."

"Just because they looked different?" Mattias asked.

"It was considered normal back then," said Sandra. "But Rosa Parks didn't want to give up her seat. She refused to get up that day when a white person wanted to sit where she had been sitting. The driver stopped the bus, called the police, and she was arrested and put in jail."

"Wow, just for sitting on a bus."

"Just for sitting on the bus," she said. "So this didn't make the other black people in Montgomery very happy, and they decided to boycott the bus system until the law was changed and they could sit in the same places as white people on the bus. Then a local pastor named Dr. Martin Luther King Jr. helped organize them, and spoke on their behalf to people in charge of the laws."

"And then they changed the laws?" Mattias asked.

"It took some time," she said, "but they changed."

"How did Rosa Parks know all of that would happen?"

"She didn't, really. In fact, there had been other African-Americans before her who had refused to follow the same laws, and they got arrested, but nothing more happened."

"How come?"

"Well," said Sandra, "I guess the time just wasn't right. People weren't ready to make the change then. But when they were, God used people like Rosa Parks and Dr. King to change history, hopefully forever."

Nearly everyone admires King and Parks today; there's not so much love for the bus driver who called the cops on her, or the ministers who spoke out in favor of segregation. History does not look favorably on King's killer, or the legislators who sought to block such laws from being overturned. History has a short memory for the others, too, who were equally committed to the same causes as King, but who lived in times or places unprepared to hear them.

We would all love to be recognized for such noble achievements. Who wouldn't want to be remembered for their acts of valor, to be recognized with monuments constructed in tribute for their contribution to humankind?

The problem is that this is what our churches have become in far too many cases: monuments to commemorate our existence, the thing by which our efforts will be remembered and appreciated. No one wants to be forgotten. The idea of disappearing from the world's collective memory is unsettling. But this is not the call of the Christian faith. Rather, we're challenged to set our egos aside, to prepare the way for something new, to usher in renewed creation, intent on reconciling all of the brokenness in our midst.

The good news is that we can do something about this. First, all Christians should engage in humble confession. We must admit when we as individuals, as Christians, and as the Church, have hurt others, whether intended or not. Second, we should ask ourselves whether our ideology is more or less important than the people and relationships with whom we share them.

Finally, and perhaps most important, we have to consider with discerning hearts and a critical eye what purpose we believe the Church and our faith are meant to serve in our world. Whereas the principal focus of our religion historically has been to win converts and save souls, there is a movement taking place in which followers of Christ lean less on propositional, rhetorical claims of faith and public rituals, opting instead to focus on the daily walk, replicating in acts both great and small the life and teachings of Jesus as we come to understand them. We remain open to the wonderful prospect of that understanding changing, too, not just through Sunday sermons or Bible studies, but even in our daily contact with others, Christian or not.

The prophet Isaiah cheered the prospect of God doing something new with us.[7] The book of Lamentations holds up the tirelessness of God's grace and compassion being made new every morning.[8] In Psalms, the author sings something new to celebrate hope for the future.[9] Jesus reminds us not to hold on to our temples and to stop worrying so much about what's going to happen next. And yet, we fall into the same trap as Peter did, trying to capture a moment and possess it as ours. We dig in, planting stakes in the ground and isolating ourselves, high on a mountain—or perhaps within our church walls—from the outside world.[10] But this isn't what Jesus wants. He calls us out of isolation, beyond the walls of religion, and into active, daily relationship and covenant with all of our brothers and sisters.

There are those who believe that their legacy is inextricably bound to the institutional Church. For those who are convinced that the Christian faith and the religious institution are essential to each other, it is hard—if not impossible—to imagine Christianity carrying on without it. There are others, pressing against the walls from the outside, hoping to see them crumble for good. Both see themselves on the right side of history, doing the work of God, or at least attempting to undo some of the less noble efforts of humanity.

There are times of great, seismic shifts throughout recorded history, but there are also great spans of time about which we know relatively little. It was sobering when I read in a book by Kester Brewin that there were about four centuries between the time when the book of Malachi (the final Old Testament book) and the Gospel of Mark (the earliest New Testament text) were written. We'll never know what happened in the in-between time, how many people lived and died, how many fought for justice, and how many resisted it. But even in their anonymity, they are a part of our still-developing story.

Those who want to make a case for the necessity of maintaining the institutional Church can find it. Those who look for evidence of the damage that same system has wrought on humanity will find plenty, too, and can make a compelling argument for burning it all down and starting over. And we do both, ironically, in the name of God and what we believe is right.

Meanwhile, something calls us forward. Toward what, we're not entirely sure. It's a story only partially written and still in progress.

Our business is to seek with an open heart and eager mind, every day, what it is that we have been created to be. We will screw it up, more than once, to be sure. We will hurt one another in the process. We will have our hearts broken, our fingers stepped on, and at times it will seem as if we're on the outside of it all. We will feel like we're stumbling around in an empty room, surrounded by four unforgiving walls.

And every so often, when the fog lifts and our path is clearly laid out before us, we take a step, maybe two, and ask, with every tentative move, "What's next?"

I can't wait to find out together.

ACKNOWLEDGMENTS

This project truly was a team effort. It would not be anywhere near the book it is today without the minds, hearts, support, love, and encouragement of so many people.

Thanks to Wendy Grisham, Kathy Helmers, Chelsea Apple, and Adrienne Ingrum for helping me beat this granite slab of an idea until it yielded a voice, a vision, and a heart.

Thanks to Marvin Read and Russ White for arguing that I could when I was sure I couldn't.

Thanks to my loving and perennially supportive wife, Amy Piatt, for making room in our lives for writing: my muse, my mistress, my selfish lover, who wakes me up nights and keeps me at the computer hours longer than I should, to wrestle the perfect word onto the page and pin it down in its proper place until it submits.

And thanks to my son, Mattias, and my daughter, Zoe, for crawling up in my lap and asking about my work, rather than resenting the time I spend gazing at a lifeless screen, rather than into their beautiful, forgiving eyes.

Notes

Chapter One: Lions and Lambs

1. Barna Group, "How Post-Christian Is America?" April 15, 2013. https://www.barna.org/barna-update/culture/608-hpca#.UnFGnZRgYmM.
2. Jeremy Weber Christian Century website, "15 Measurements of Whether Americans Are Post-Christian," April 15, 2013. http://www.christianitytoday.com/gleanings/2013/april/15-measurements-of-whether-americans-are-post-christian.html.

Chapter Two: The Gospel According to Kerouac

1. Jeff Hawkins with Sandra Blakeslee, *On Intelligence*. Times Books/Henry Holt and Company, 2005, p. 89.
2. In the original text, this word appeared as "toward," though it seems that it was meant to read "reward." I have corrected it within the citation, given that assumption. David Rock, "A Hunger for Certainty," *Psychology Today* website, October 25, 2009. http://www.psychologytoday.com/blog/your-brain-work/200910/hunger-certainty.
3. Graeme Wood, "Anthropology Inc.," *Atlantic Monthly*, March 2013. http://www.theatlantic.com/magazine/archive/2013/03/anthropology-inc/309218/.
4. National Public Radio website, "In Constant Digital Contact, We Feel 'Alone Together'" October 17, 2012. http://www.npr.org/2012/10/18/163098594/in-constant-digital-contact-we-feel-alone-together.
5. Acts 2.

Chapter Three: Then Comes the Fall

1. Bart D. Ehrman, *Lost Christianities: The Battles for Scripture*

and the Faiths We Never Knew. Oxford University Press, 2004, pp. 2–4.

2. Ibid.

3. Ibid., pp. 135–36.

4. Ibid., p. 249.

5. Dale B. Martin, "The Last Trumpet: 'Revelations,' by Elaine Pagels, *The New York Times*, April 6, 2012. http://www.ny times.com/2012/04/08/books/review/revelations-by-elaine-pag els.html?pagewanted=all&_r=0.

6. Proverbs 16:16–19.

7. Desiring God website, "What Made It Okay for God to Kill Woman and Children in the Old Testament?" February 27, 2012. http://www.desiringgod.org/resource-library/ask-pastor -john/what-made-it-ok-for-god-to-kill-women-and-children-in -the-old-testament.

8. Hans Johnson and William Iskridge, "The Legacy of Falwell's Bully Pulpit—A Commentary by William Iskridge, '78," *The Washington Post*, May 19, 2007. http://www.law.yale.edu /news/5131.htm.

9. Anne Lamott, *Bird by Bird: Some Instructions on Writing and Life*. Anchor, 1995.

CHAPTER FOUR: SPEAKING SILENTLY

1. Matthew 15:21–28.

2. John D. Caputo, "For Love of the Things Themselves: Derrida's Hyper-Realism," in *On Realism*, a special issue of *Social Semiotics*, vol. 11, no. 1, 2001, Guest Editor Niall Lucy. http://www.jcrt.org/archives/01.3/caputo.shtml.

3. John D. Caputo, *The Insistence of God: A Theology of Perhaps*. Indiana University Press, 2013. http://www.iupress.indiana.edu /product_info.php?cPath=6040_1152&products_id=806898.

4. Gianni Vattimo, John D. Caputo, and Jeffrey W. Robbins, *After the Death of God (Insurrections: Critical Studies in Religion, Politics, and Culture)*. Columbia University Press, 2009, p. 65.

Chapter Five: House of Cards

1. Roland Bainton, *Hunted Heretic: The Life and Death of Michael Servetus (1511–1553)*. Blackstone Editions, 2005, p. 107.
2. Ibid., p. 141.
3. Ibid., p. 146.
4. Melanie Nathan, "Bullied Gay Teen's Suicide Note," San Diego Gay & Lesbian News website. http://sdgln.com/news/2012/01/26/bullied-gay-teen-suicide-note-insight-ericjames-borges-death 19#sthash.n2P6cJZF.dpbs.
5. Matthew 3:7–9.
6. Matthew 5:20.
7. Matthew 22: 34–40.
8. Mark 12:28–34.

Chapter Six: Life on a Flat Planet

1. Mark 5:34.
2. Mark 10:52.
3. Luke 7:50.
4. Luke 17:19.
5. Søren Kierkegaard, *Concluding Unscientific Postscript to Philosophical Fragments*. Princeton University Press, 1992, p. 382.

Chapter Seven: From Breast to Cross

1. David Gibson, "Christmas' Missing Icon: The Breastfeeding Jesus," December 11, 2012. The Christian Century website. http://www.christiancentury.org/article/2012-12/christmas-missing-icon-mary-breastfeeding-jesus.
2. Augustine of Hippo, *Confessions*, 8:17.
3. Rita Nakashima Brock and Rebecca Ann Parker, *Saving Paradise: How Christianity Traded Love of This World for Crucifixion and Empire*. Beacon Press, 2009, p. 300.

4. Ibid., p. 301.
5. Sex Addiction Rehab website, "3 Jobs Commonly Linked to Sex Addiction." http://www.sexaddictionrehab.org/3-jobs-common ly-linked-to-sex-addiction/.

CHAPTER EIGHT: RE-MEMBERING

1. Mark Nepo, *The Book of Awakening: Having the Life You Want by Being Present to the Life You Have.* Conari Press, 2011, p. 419.

CHAPTER NINE: A GAMBLER'S EMPIRE

1. 3 John 1:2 (KJV).
2. "Changing Faiths: Latinos and the Transformation of American Religion," Pew Center for Hispanic Studies, p. 32.
3. Simon Coleman, *The Globalisation of Charismatic Christianity: Spreading the Gospel of Prosperity.* Cambridge University Press, 2000, p. 28.
4. Hanna Rosin, "Did Christianity Cause the Crash?" *The Atlantic,* December 2009. www.theatlantic.com/magazine/archive /2009/12/did-christianity-cause-the-crash/307764/.
5. Ibid.
6. Jackson Lears, *Something for Nothing: Luck in America.* Viking Adult, 2003, p. 14.
7. Demographia website, "Debt to Income Ratios: United States 1980–2006." http://www.demographia.com/db-usdebtratio -history.pdf.
8. Rosin, "Did Christianity Cause the Crash?"
9. Ibid.
10. Ibid.
11. Kate Bowler, *Blessed: A History of the American Prosperity Gospel.* Oxford University Press, 2013, p. 99.
12. Luiza Oleszczuk, "US Megachurches, Hundreds of Christians Targeted in Ponzi Scheme?" *Christian Post,* April 13, 2012. http://www.christianpost.com/news/us-megachurches-hundreds

-of-christians-targeted-in-ponzi-scheme-73181/.

13. Ibid.

14. Pew Research Religion & Public Life Project, "Religious Landscape Survey." http://religions.pewforum.org/reports.

CHAPTER TEN: HUNGRY AS DOGS

1. David Moore, "We Are Not Who You Think We Are," Speech addressing the Black History Assembly, February 11, 2013. http://www.youtube.com/watch?feature=player_embedded&v =TpE_z8A8AHk.

2. Editorial, "The Price of Hunger," *Los Angeles Times*, June 23, 2008. http://articles.latimes.com/2008/jun/23/opinion/ed-food23.

3. "The Catholic Church in America: Earthly Concerns," *The Economist*, August 18, 2012. http://www.economist.com /node/21560536.

4. David Briggs, "The Flesh is Weak: Churchgoers Give Far Less Than They Think," *The Huffington Post*, September 1, 2012. http://www.huffingtonpost.com/david-briggs/the-flesh-is-weak-c hurchgoers-give-far-less-than-they-think_b_1846516.html.

CHAPTER ELEVEN: IF ONLY THEY WERE (FILL IN THE BLANK)

1. World Christian Database. www.intervarsity.org/ism/article /1768.

2. Catechism of the Catholic Church: III, "The Love of Husband and Wife." Section 2370.

3. Exodus 21:24.

4. Luke 15:11–32.

5. Genesis 11:1–9.

6. Acts 2:1–13.

7. Genesis 5:32–10:1 (NRSV).

CHAPTER TWELVE: NINJA JESUS

1. Walter Wink, *Jesus and Nonviolence: A Third Way*. Fortress Press, 2003, p. 45.

CHAPTER THIRTEEN: MILLIONS IN THE HANDS OF AN ANGRY GOD

1. "American Piety in the 21st Century: New Insights to the Depth and Complexity of Religion in the US." Selected Findings from the Baylor Religion Survey, September 2006. http://www.baylor.edu/content/services/document.php/33304.pdf.
2. Kevin J. Flannelly et al., "Beliefs, Mental Health and Evolutionary Threat Assessment Systems in the Brain," *Journal of Nervous & Mental Disease*, December 2007, vol. 195, Issue 12, pp. 996–1003.
3. Ross Pomeroy, "Belief in Angry God Associated with Poor Mental Health," *Real Clear Science*, April 16, 2013. http://www.realclearscience.com/blog/2013/04/belief-in-punitive-god-associated-with-poor-mental-health.html.
4. N. R. Silton, K. J. Flannelly, K. Galek, and C. G. Ellison, "Beliefs About God and Mental Health Among American Adults," *Journal of Religious Health*, April 10, 2013.
5. K. Flannelly, K. Galek, C. Ellison, and H. Koenig, "Beliefs About God, Psychiatric Symptoms, and Evolutionary Psychiatry," *Journal of Religion and Health*, 2009.
6. Kathleen Galek and Matthew Porter, "A Brief Review of Religious Beliefs in Research on Mental Health and ETAS Theory," *Journal of Health Care Chaplaincy*, vol. 16, 2010, pp. 58–64.

CHAPTER FOURTEEN: CARRYING EACH OTHER

1. Brene Brown, "Listening to Shame," TED Talks, March 2012. http://www.ted.com/talks/brene_brown_listening_to_shame.html.
2. Matthew 18:20 (NRSV).

CHAPTER FIFTEEN: TYRANNY OF THE UN-POSSESSED

1. Rene Girard, *Deceit, Desire and the Novel: Self and Other in Literary Structure.* Johns Hopkins University Press, 1976, p. 101.
2. Henri J. M. Nouwen, *Making All Things New: An Invitation to the Spiritual Life.* HarperOne, 1981.
3. Luke 22:42.

CHAPTER SEVENTEEN: WHICH SIDE OF HISTORY?

1. Mark 13:32.
2. Mark 13:2.
3. "Bible Verses About Refiners Fire," The Official King James Bible Online, http://www.kingjamesbibleonline.org/Bible-Verses -About-Refiners-Fire/.
4. Genesis 3:19.
5. Romans 8:1–17, *The Message,* interpretation of the Bible by Eugene Peterson.
6. Rev. Phil Snider's entire speech can be found at http://www.youtube.com/watch?v=A8JsRx2lois.
7. Isaiah 43:19.
8. Lamentations 3:22–23.
9. Psalm 40.
10. Matthew 17:1–9.

ABOUT THE AUTHOR

Christian Piatt had a Bible (literally) thrown at him when he was kicked out of his youth group for asking too many questions about God, about Jesus, and about the Christian faith that he would end up running from for much of his life. After painstakingly regaining his faith, this author, speaker, musician, spoken word artist, and editor has discovered a platform to help reconcile what Christianity claims to be with what it's intended to be. Piatt's words speak to a generation of people who are defecting from religion in response to years of hypocrisy and abuse.

Christian is the creator and editor of the Banned Questions book series, which include *Banned Questions About the Bible*, *Banned Questions About Jesus*, and *Banned Questions About Christians*. He co-created and co-edited the WTF: Where's the Faith? young adult series with Chalice Press, for which he also co-edited the book *Split Ticket: Independent Faith in a Time of Partisan Politics*, and contributed a chapter to *Oh God, Oh God, Oh God!: Young Adults Speak Out About Sexuality and Christianity*.

Christian's first book, *LOST: A Search for Meaning*, came out in 2006, followed by *MySpace to Sacred Space: God for a New Generation* in 2007, which was coauthored with Amy. In 2012, Chalice Press published his memoir on faith, family, and parenting called *PregMANcy: A Dad, a Little Dude and a Due Date*. He published his first novel, *Blood Doctrine*, in 2014.

In addition to his books, Christian is a contributor to the *Huffington Post*, a blogger for *Patheos*, and a contributing writer for *Sojourners* and *Red Letter Christians*, among others.